Complimentary Copy

START AND RUN A PROFITABLE STUDENT-RUN BUSINESS

DISCARD

START AND RUN A PROFITABLE STUDENT-RUN BUSINESS
Your step-by-step plan for turning bright ideas into big bucks

David Schincariol

Self-Counsel Press
(a division of)
International Self-Counsel Press Ltd.
Canada   U.S.A.

Printed in Canada

First edition: August, 1995

Canadian Cataloguing in Publication Data

Schincariol, David, 1972-
    Start and run a profitable student-run business

    (Self-counsel business series)
    ISBN 1-55180-026-8

    1. Student-owned business enterprises — Management. 2. New business enterprises — Management. I. Title. II. Series.
HD62.5.S34 1995   658.1'1'024375   C95-910394-5

Cover photography by Terry Guscott, ATN Visuals, Vancouver, B.C.

Self-Counsel Press
(a division of)
International Self-Counsel Press Ltd.

Head and Editorial Office	*U.S. Address*
1481 Charlotte Road	1704 N. State Street
North Vancouver, British Columbia	Bellingham, Washington
Canada V7J 1H1	U.S.A. 98225

This book is dedicated to my parents and grandparents in appreciation for their encouragement and assistance over the years, particularly Maria Schincariol, for instilling in me the value of initiative and having faith in my abilities.

CONTENTS

TABLES

SAMPLES

CHECKLISTS

WORKSHEETS

ACKNOWLEDGMENTS

Special thanks to Jeff Whiting, my sister Lisa, and my friends and mentors for their encouragement, support, advice, and suggestions.

In addition, I wish to acknowledge the valuable training, resources and/or guidance of College Pro Painters, the Ontario Ministry of Economic Development & Trade, the University of Toronto, and the Royal Bank.

INTRODUCTION

Until recently, starting a business was considered an extremely risky undertaking to be considered only by those with experience. Today, many people are taking responsibility for their own employment by creating their own jobs. Government planners predict that new and small businesses will continue to provide the majority of new jobs; there is no doubt that a business start-up represents exciting opportunities. Each year, short-term, part-time, or seasonal business start-ups outnumber permanent businesses. Students are the major initiators of this type of business.

This book is a general introduction to starting and running a business at the student level. It is suitable for any reader, regardless of education or business experience. It provides a step-by-step guide for the generation, creation, and management of your own business idea.

The first two chapters help you evaluate potential new business ideas to set you on the right path for business start-up. Chapter 3 discusses franchising and why it can be a worthwhile opportunity for student entrepreneurs. Chapters 4 to 6 explain different possible business structures and also how to set up your business and create a business plan. Chapters 7 to 10 help you find financing for your idea, suppliers, and contacts, as well as discuss quick, inexpensive advertising options for your business. Chapter 11 explains how to price your product or estimate your service to land as many profitable jobs as possible. Chapters 12 to 15 explain the technical side of setting up your business, such as accounting, taxes, managing employees, and dealing with your competition. Chapter 16 offers timesaving tricks of the trade to help you balance school and business. Chapter 17 provides helpful contacts, including educational, student entrepreneurial groups, and networking connections. Finally, chapter 18 is a detailed problem and solution guide to help you through the potential difficulties many student entrepreneurs encounter.

Sample forms, tables, worksheets, and checklists have been included for practical use when developing and running your business. Additionally, the Appendix lists contacts for further business education as well as where to go for the answers to specific questions.

Follow each chapter as you develop your business idea, especially if this is your first business start-up. Those already in business will find this book a key management and troubleshooting tool.

Owning your own business is a great job. It offers you challenge, freedom, and new opportunities. It helps you develop your confidence, your organizational skills, and build your bank account.

Read on, and good luck with your new enterprise!

1
RUNNING YOUR OWN BUSINESS

Running your own student business can be profitable and educational. There are two things students must consider before striking out on their own. First, starting a business is not the answer for everyone. Before you strike out on your own, consider what's involved. You need to determine if running your own business will help you attain your goals and make money.

Second, a student business can be developed on virtually any scale. As student entrepreneurs, we are not expected to immediately create a fast-growing software giant such as Microsoft (although that would be nice!). Nor is it necessary that we employ a lot of people. Starting your own business might mean painting houses on your own, running a large landscaping company, promoting yourself as a consultant, or managing a group of lifeguards to teach swimming lessons. Anything is possible.

You can build a profitable business around an interest or skill. Owning your own business can give you the opportunity to make money in a field you're interested in. As a student, you may not get this chance when you work for others.

Therefore, choose a business that interests you, that you have some knowledge about, and that fills a specific niche. Following are possible product-based and service-based businesses that are well-suited to the student entrepreneur who wants seasonal or part-time work. Many of these types of businesses are already being run by students and have proven to be successful.

Some ideas for *product-based* student businesses:

- Selling used computers
- Planting trees
- Selling Christmas trees
- Selling comic books
- Running a small fast-food restaurant and/or delivery
- Selling appliances door to door
- Running a craft-based business
- Selling stained glass windows
- Flower import and distribution
- Poster and art distribution
- Publishing magazines
- Making patio furniture
- Opening a bakery
- Selling chocolates, pastries, pies
- Making documentaries
- Reselling fire and security alarms
- Reselling hobby-related equipment
- Selling health foods
- Selling eaves troughing
- Designing kids' clothing
- Marketing clothing
- Reselling other manufacturers' products such as pool chemicals, lawn care products, windows
- Selling marketing products such as posters
- Running a rental company
- Developing and marketing computer software

- Developing recycling products
- Developing new innovative products such as the better mousetrap, the better garden composter, or the better car alarm

This list represents only a small and general sample of possible business ideas that suit students. Don't limit yourself to this list; there are many more niche businesses that are great for students even though they are typically thought of as full-time businesses.

Some ideas for possible *service-based* student businesses:

- Painting houses
- Installing underground sprinklers
- Promoting events
- Landscaping
- Creating an independent record label
- Teaching private swimming lessons
- Conducting tours
- Removing garbage
- Recycling services
- Building decks
- Building fences
- Delivering groceries
- Office maintenance
- Computer consulting
- Tree planting
- Installing security alarms
- Installing car stereo systems
- Pet grooming
- Pet-sitting
- Teaching skiing
- Teaching tennis
- Interior design
- Office design
- Teaching a musical instrument
- Repairing glass and mirrors
- Installing interlocking brick
- Tutoring services

- Cleaning eaves troughs
- Bakery services
- Maid service
- Cutting lawns
- Light construction (sheds, basement remodeling)
- Photography studio

These are only a few of the many business ventures that students can launch. Be creative; look at what interests you and don't be put off by thinking that only full-time businesses can succeed. There are peak and seasonal times for any business. Find the one that suits you and your schedule.

a. ADVANTAGES AND DISADVANTAGES OF RUNNING YOUR OWN BUSINESS

1. Advantages

(a) *You are the boss:* You are in control of what goes on, when, and where. It's your show! You don't take orders from anyone. You do things your way. It is up to you to balance that freedom with your responsibility to your business.

(b) *You can have unlimited earnings:* Unlike a conventional job, you have no set pay rate. If you work successfully on your own you can make much more than your usual $7 an hour. Your time and effort pay off far more in the long run and you are more appreciated for the skills that you, as an individual, have to offer.

(c) *You set the working hours:* You work as long as you want, when you want. You are not enslaved to working certain, often inconvenient, shifts. Students can fit their business in between classes during early afternoons and weekends. These intangible advantages make a big difference to the bottom line.

(d) *You enjoy a sense of achievement:* You have the opportunity of building something big from scratch. If your business succeeds, it's your doing. You can fulfill your goal to be a successful individual and learn a great deal in the process.

(e) *You can work at something that you are interested in:* You can start your own business in any field you want. If you pick a hobby or particular interest, it can make every workday fun. If you enjoy your business, it could grow into a full-time career.

2. Disadvantages

(a) *You risk losing time and money:* In the worst case, if your business is not successful, you risk losing your personal investment of time and money. You may spend most of your time working to make back your losses if your business venture does not succeed.

(b) *You may worry and experience stress:* Unlike a regular job, you cannot go home at the end of your shift and forget about the problems at work. As well, problems at work are *your* problems, since you own the business and you have to be the one to deal with them.

(c) *You may have to work long hours:* Many business owners work as many as 60 hours a week. You cannot leave your business problems behind you when you quit working for the day. You take them home and work on them in your head even when you are trying to relax.

(d) *You need to understand and be proficient in a number of areas:* In a normal job, you only need to know how to do the tasks involved in doing your particular job. As a small business owner you must be able to manage people, finances, and marketing. You must also have a good understanding of all the tasks involved in producing your product or service.

(e) *You must be self-starting:* In your own business no one is going to force you to go to work or to put forth the effort needed to earn money. If you don't get yourself up and going every day you will not be successful.

As you can see, there are advantages and disadvantages to running your own business. By following this book carefully and by planning and managing your new business well, you will minimize the effect any disadvantages may have and maximize all the advantages. To be successful, you've got to plan properly and expect to put in a great deal of effort before you start getting anything in return. However, the benefits of successful planning and persistent effort pay off far beyond what you can make at the typical summer or part-time student job.

b. YOU AND YOUR SKILLS

Listed below are a number of personal characteristics that business professionals and others have shown are necessary for entrepreneurial success. Worksheet #1 helps you evaluate your strengths and weaknesses. It also gives you an idea of what skills you possess and what skills you need to locate in other people or resources. In general, this test should give you some idea of your potential entrepreneurial ability.

The purpose of the test is to establish your particular entrepreneurial strengths and weaknesses, so think carefully about your answers and be as honest as you can. Since each person has his or her own strengths and weaknesses, it's unlikely that anyone would select "very high" for all the personality traits. However, it is important to understand how important these traits are in making business decisions and managing people. Once you know where your strengths and weaknesses lie, you can

PERSONALITY TRAIT

Goal oriented

How important is it to you that you achieve your goals? Do you frequently pursue tasks by setting goals?

Very High	High	Average	Low	Very Low
❑	❑	❑	❑	❑

Ability to be self-starting

How strong is your willingness to strike out and make your ideas reality? Do you need to be pushed into starting an activity or are you off and running on your own?

Very High	High	Average	Low	Very Low
❑	❑	❑	❑	❑

Commitment

How prepared are you to put a great deal of effort into your business?

Very High	High	Average	Low	Very Low
❑	❑	❑	❑	❑

Decision-making ability

How high is your ability to make decisions quickly and effectively with confidence?

Very High	High	Average	Low	Very Low
❑	❑	❑	❑	❑

Problem-solving ability

How great is your ability and willingness to recognize, assess, and actively tackle problems which may come up in both your personal life and in your business?

Very High	High	Average	Low	Very Low
❑	❑	❑	❑	❑

Ability to deal with stress

Can you continue to work effectively under stress? Do you thrive on stress?

Very High	High	Average	Low	Very Low
❑	❑	❑	❑	❑

Ability to network and use feedback

What is your understanding of the importance and usefulness of other people's skills, education, and experience? Do you feel that you have the ability to learn from them to improve your activities?

Very High	High	Average	Low	Very Low
❑	❑	❑	❑	❑

Integrity

Do you have high personal standards? Do you believe in high-quality business?

Very High	High	Average	Low	Very Low
❑	❑	❑	❑	❑

Ability to analyze opportunities

Can you effectively analyze business opportunities? Do you feel comfortable risking money and time on researched ventures with uncertain returns?

Very High	High	Average	Low	Very Low
❑	❑	❑	❑	❑

Self-awareness

How well do you know your strengths and weaknesses? Do you have the ability to look realistically at new ideas?

Very High	High	Average	Low	Very Low
❑	❑	❑	❑	❑

Ability to deal with frustration

Can you take 60 noes and keep trying? Can you continually work toward a goal despite difficulties that may arise?

Very High	High	Average	Low	Very Low
❑	❑	❑	❑	❑

Ability to deal with problems and failure

Can you use problems and failures as learning experiences to help you understand and create better ways of doing things in order to avoid problems in the future?

Very High	High	Average	Low	Very Low
❑	❑	❑	❑	❑

Interpersonal Skills

Can you be a team builder and lead a group of people to realize your goals? How do you perceive your ability to produce positive interactions between customers, suppliers, or anyone needing to associate with the business?

Very High	High	Average	Low	Very Low
❑	❑	❑	❑	❑

consider how you can compensate for any shortcomings. On a separate sheet, make a list of your top five strengths and weaknesses, based on your test.

The challenge now is to decide what kind of business will let you use those strengths most effectively and to consider how you can improve any weaknesses. There are all kinds of resources, books, and people you can talk to about self-improvement. It's important to be aware of your personal weaknesses from the start. People in business have to make decisions and take risks every day. Part of the challenge of starting a business is being able to learn from your mistakes. Recognize that you have difficulty making decisions or that you're afraid to take risks, and keep this in mind when you have to negotiate with suppliers or deal with employees.

c. THE KEY INGREDIENTS FOR A SUCCESSFUL STUDENT BUSINESS

What will make your business successful depends a lot on who you are and what kind of business you decide to start. However, the success of every student business depends on these five key ingredients:

    (a) The ability to be self-starting and hard working

    (b) Maintaining your confidence despite difficulties which may arise

    (c) Thorough knowledge of your field of business

    (d) Stressing service, quality, reliability, and cost-effectiveness in your business dealings

    (e) Effective planning

1. Be self-starting and hard working

Make your business successful by out-competing your competitors. Take time to do things right: Listen to your customers and answer their questions. Take time to look for new customers and never forego an opportunity to make a business contact. A few hours spent calling back potential customers or looking for new ones can make an immeasurable difference to your profit margin. It may sound like a lot for a student to take on, but with proper time management for all your tasks, all you need is the initiative to follow through.

As a student you have a flexible schedule; use this to your advantage. Chapter 16 helps you plan out your school, business, and social activities so that you can incorporate all of them into your new lifestyle. Start planning early and organize your time effectively from day one. If you leave time organization until you get really busy it will be too late to catch up.

2. Be confident despite difficulties which may arise

Surveys suggest that confidence really does breed success. When you are dealing with business problems, DON'T LET YOURSELF BECOME DISCOURAGED. Tackle problems one by one and constantly think of solutions, not problems. If you really believe it will work, you will find a way to make it work. If you really believe it will fail, you will be less likely to find solutions.

As well, if you are confident when you deal with employees and customers, they will feel confident about dealing with you. If you are constantly unsure of yourself, others will not be as likely to believe in you or want to invest their time and money in your endeavors. However, be prepared if your business does not work out. Try not to burn your bridges with other employment possibilities and don't overcommit your personal resources even if you really believe it will work.

3. Know your field of business

When creating and running your business, draw on your background. Education or even hobbies are skills to build a business around. They ensure your knowledge of the business, its pitfalls, and areas of opportunity. Furthermore, it makes your business an enjoyable place to spend your time and energy.

4. Stress service, quality, reliability, and cost-effectiveness

Customers are concerned about price. However, if a customer is concerned about service, quality, or reliability they are much less apt to buy your product or service, regardless of price. This is particularly true in a student business since many customers may be concerned that a student cannot do as good a job as a professional or a full-time person. So price competitively, but emphasize service, quality, and reliability.

5. Plan

Use this book to think through your business ideas, to set goals, and to ensure that you really understand what's going on. Set goals and work toward them one by one. The best way to be successful is to start out knowing what success is and how to get it. To do this you have to map out your goals and decide how you will reach them. This will bring you a sense of success. Chapters 4 and 5 help you set goals, evaluate your market, and plan for success.

Following are some facts and figures on student businesses and student entrepreneurs based on government and private sector surveys.

STUDENT BUSINESS STATISTICS

- It has been estimated that as many as one in four students start some form of a business during their school years.

- In a survey on why students wanted to start businesses, 48% said to make money, 20% wanted to be their own boss, 17% wanted a sense of accomplishment, and 10% cited other reasons.

- Of the long-term plans of students who started businesses, 33% wanted to run their own business, 22% were undecided, and 45% wanted future employment by someone else.

- The distribution of student businesses by industry: manufacturing 3%, retail 16%, and service 81%.

- The level of education most student entrepreneurs pursued: secondary school 24%, college 15%, university 61%.

- Most student entrepreneurs find funding from relatives or friends and generally do not take out business loans. In fact, as few as 10% get loans from banks.

- When run independently, about 65% of student businesses are successful at meeting or exceeding their goals in the first year. When students run a reputable franchise, well over 90% are successful.

2
NEW BUSINESS IDEAS

From the first chapter, you can now see that, for the right personality, becoming an entrepreneur is not such an impossible task. There are tremendous business opportunities available to students with initiative, skill, and interest.

You have already taken the initiative to go ahead and start planning your business and you know what business skills and interests you have. The next step is to find a business idea that is right for you and can be made profitable with your skills, education, and funding. Consider the following:

(a) *Your skills:* Decide what your skills are and look for a business that allows you to combine and market them in an interesting way. Will you enjoy this business?

(b) *The level of financial investment required:* This includes any start-up costs, legal fees, and inventory costs. What funds are available to you? A business with minimal overhead and resalable fixed assets is best for most student entrepreneurs.

(c) *Time commitment and when you can spare it:* Are you a morning or night person? Do you mind working weekends? It is very important that you not grow to resent what you are doing and be burned-out by the time you return to school. A business with variable hours is best for most students.

(d) *Your abilities and willingness to manage people:* Does your business require employees or can you run it yourself?

(e) *Short start-up time:* Since this business will probably be your only source of income and you may only be running it seasonally or part-time, you want to start getting a return from your business quickly.

(f) *Will this business provide you with the income you want or need for school?* You should be sure that your projected sales are reasonable for you to make enough income in the time your business is operating. Consider a cash-only business to help avoid long payback periods and the risk of bad debts.

(g) *Location and transportation:* Do you live far away and need to buy a vehicle, or could you use someone else's car or live at home?

(h) *Are you comfortable dealing with people in a business setting?* If not, consider a business with limited personal contact or one that will allow you to hire employees to do the direct selling.

(i) *Does your business require special training?* Certain industries have government regulations. Contact a local small business office listed in the Appendix for specific information on your business type.

(j) *Future potential of your new business idea:* You will be putting long hours into developing your business and you may want to continue it in future years. Is the market expanding or decreasing for your product or service? Is your business idea a passing fad that may fade away in a few years or months?

a. PURSUING YOUR NEW BUSINESS IDEA

As a student entrepreneur, you have three choices for starting your own business. You can start your business completely from scratch, you can buy a franchise operation, or you can buy an existing business. Each choice has its advantages and disadvantages.

1. Starting from scratch vs. buying a franchise or an existing business

The advantages when you start your business from scratch are the following:

(a) *Your initial start-up costs are low:* Compared to buying a business or franchise, the start-up costs of a new business are basically whatever you decide to put into it.

(b) *You are free to sell any product or service wherever you want:* Unlike a franchise, you have no sales territory and unlike an established business, you have no previous expectations or set customer base and are able to sell to any customers you can find.

(c) *The success of the business is entirely your accomplishment:* Starting a business from scratch is not only great experience to put on your resume, but is also personally rewarding.

(d) *The education gained in starting your own business is invaluable:* This knowledge and experience is useful to you far beyond operating your own business. It can help

open the door to many future career opportunities.

(e) *There is the potential to attract customers from a new niche:* Unlike the predetermined marketing approach of a franchise or existing business, when you set up a new business, you are free to find the segment of the market that the competition hasn't penetrated. This gives your business the potential to be far more profitable than a franchise or existing business.

The disadvantages to starting from scratch are the following:

(a) *You lack an established reputation for your product or service:* It is your responsibility to build a name and public image for your company. There is no established customer base or advertised name to build on, as is the case in a franchise or existing business.

(b) *You must find suppliers:* It is your job to find and establish supplier accounts and this takes time and money. As part of a franchise, all of the decisions about which supplier to use have already been made for you.

(c) *You must find customers:* It is your job to find and establish a market and you have to take the time and money to do this. You will not have any prior goodwill or company awareness to help you.

(d) *It may be difficult for you to get a loan:* Due to the newness and unproven track record of your new business idea you may find it difficult to get loans from your bank.

Although most people think starting a business is a good idea, a student entrepreneur may find that starting a business from scratch is too hard. Either way, weigh the alternatives before you forge ahead.

Most student entrepreneurs will start a part-time or seasonal business, so a franchise opportunity or starting a new business are options if you want to keep costs low. Depending on your previous experience and the type of business you want to run, one will have advantages over the other. Chapter 3 helps you assess possible franchise ideas.

If you decide to start a new business from scratch, read on. Read this chapter carefully along with chapter 3 so that you can assess your business idea and choose the business that is best suited to you.

b. GETTING YOUR BUSINESS IDEA

The first step is to choose an idea. Look for products or services that fit into a niche. Who is the market for that product or service? Is there a way to market your idea differently so that you can reach or meet the needs of part of that market? For example, let's say that you want to teach swimming lessons and you have a backyard pool or access to one. There are other organizations and instructors out there already teaching swimming lessons, so you need to be better, special, more accessible, or cheaper. One way to set your business apart from the others would be to offer private swimming lessons in the clients' own pool, or in your pool if clients don't have a pool, at the same cost or cheaper, with the promise of more friendly and individualized service. As a student, you have the advantage of flexibility. Use it!

Use Worksheet #2 to help you assess your interests and skills. Think of your interests or skills as a potential new business. Using them as a base for your business will make your business more enjoyable and, since you are already interested in it, will ensure that you really know your field or industry. Look for aspects of your hobbies or education that you could develop into products or services.

Nearly all of us have had good ideas for new businesses. The purpose of the following exercise is to generate as many business ideas as possible. Generate ideas; don't worry about evaluating them at this point but do try to consider personal preferences — don't put down a business idea if you know it doesn't appeal to you. Consider any open niches that you think you can fill because there is much less competition in these areas and profits can be made sooner. Use Worksheet #3 to list all the new business ideas you can come up with.

c. ASSESSING THE MARKETABILITY OF YOUR NEW BUSINESS IDEA

First, show your list of ideas to at least three people who you know will give you an honest, educated, or experienced opinion. Do they have any other ideas? Would they add or delete any items? What advantages or pitfalls do they see in particular ideas? There is no better source for idea evaluation than the opinion of others. This step will increase your potential for success dramatically and help you avoid costly and frustrating mistakes in your business start-up.

Next, take all the advice and feedback from others and make a new list of the four ideas that you think are the best. Try to think of as many advantages and disadvantages for each (see Worksheet #4); find out what other people think. Consider whether you are attracted to any of these ideas for businesses and how they match your interests. Of these four, which ones would be the most costly to set up? Which ones can be set up easily and require the least structure?

Now that you have considered all the advantages and disadvantages, decide which business ideas are your top two. Call these your "Idea Number One" and "Idea Number Two." Using the telephone directory, the Yellow Pages, other business people, and any other useful sources, find out information about specific customers, suppliers, and competitors for your business

WORKSHEET #2
PERSONAL SKILLS AND INTERESTS

1. I think my main skills are:

    1. _____

    2. _____

    3. _____

    4. _____

    5. _____

    6. _____

2. I am particularly interested in:

    1. _____

    2. _____

    3. _____

    4. _____

    5. _____

    6. _____

3. Other people think I am very good at:

    1. _____

    2. _____

    3. _____

    4. _____

    5. _____

    6. _____

Possible new business ideas:

1. _____
2. _____
3. _____
4. _____
5. _____
6. _____
7. _____
8. _____
9. _____
10. _____
11. _____
12. _____
13. _____
14. _____
15. _____
16. _____
17. _____
18. _____
19. _____
20. _____

(see Worksheet #5). Consider how you can make your service or product more attractive than the competition's. Think about where you can get inexpensive but reliable, good quality supplies, and how you will attract potential customers.

Now take your top two ideas along with the information you have gathered about customers, suppliers, and competitors and decide which one is the best idea. The best idea is generally the one for which you can accurately list a large number of specific customers, an adequate and readily available number of suppliers, and a low number of competitors. If you have thoroughly investigated what your competition is up to, you should have solid reasons for believing that you can out-compete them.

Worksheet #6 is designed to help you evaluate your new business idea. Write your new business idea at the top of Worksheet #6 and put it to the test.

WORKSHEET #4
BUSINESS IDEA EVALUATION SHEET — PART 1

IDEA	DISADVANTAGES	ADVANTAGES

1.
_____
_____
_____
_____
_____
_____

DISADVANTAGES
1._____
2._____
3._____
4._____
5._____
6._____
7._____
8._____
9._____
10._____

ADVANTAGES
1._____
2._____
3._____
4._____
5._____
6._____
7._____
8._____
9._____
10._____

2.
_____
_____
_____
_____
_____
_____

DISADVANTAGES
1._____
2._____
3._____
4._____
5._____
6._____
7._____
8._____
9._____
10._____

ADVANTAGES
1._____
2._____
3._____
4._____
5._____
6._____
7._____
8._____
9._____
10._____

IDEA	DISADVANTAGES	ADVANTAGES
3. _____ _____ _____ _____ _____ _____	1._____ 2._____ 3._____ 4._____ 5._____ 6._____ 7._____ 8._____ 9._____ 10._____	1._____ 2._____ 3._____ 4._____ 5._____ 6._____ 7._____ 8._____ 9._____ 10._____
4. _____ _____ _____ _____ _____ _____	1._____ 2._____ 3._____ 4._____ 5._____ 6._____ 7._____ 8._____ 9._____ 10._____	1._____ 2._____ 3._____ 4._____ 5._____ 6._____ 7._____ 8._____ 9._____ 10._____

Idea #1 _____

_____

Customers	Suppliers	Competitors
1._____	1._____	1._____
2._____	2._____	2._____
3._____	3._____	3._____
4._____	4._____	4._____
5._____	5._____	5._____
6._____	6._____	6._____
7._____	7._____	7._____
8._____	8._____	8._____

Idea #2 _____

_____

Customers	Suppliers	Competitors
1._____	1._____	1._____
2._____	2._____	2._____
3._____	3._____	3._____
4._____	4._____	4._____
5._____	5._____	5._____
6._____	6._____	6._____
7._____	7._____	7._____
8._____	8._____	8._____

WORKSHEET #6
HOW TO TEST YOUR IDEA

After gathering information about potential customers, suppliers, and competitors,

MY NEW BUSINESS IDEA IS:

_____

_____

Complete the questions below to see how your idea holds up. If your idea falls into one of the following categories, put a check mark in the box and add or subtract the corresponding number of points. An optimal student business idea will score 100.

Elements of a poor business idea ✓ **IF YES**

- has a high overhead ❑ -30 points

- is centered around one product or service ❑ -10 points

- has no long-term potential ❑ -10 points

- has limited growth or is outdated ❑ -20 points

- requires specialized technical experience ❑ -30 points

Elements of a good business idea ✓ **IF YES**

- has a product or service that appeals to most people ❑ +20 points

- has potential for repeat business ❑ +20 points

- has flexible hours ❑ +10 points

- has immediate income potential ❑ +20 points

- fills a niche that is currently empty or under-
  serviced or meets an identified need ❑ +30 points

_____ **TOTAL**

0 to 20	Poor idea
20 to 40	Marginal idea
40 to 60	Adequate idea
60 to 80	Good idea
80 to 100	Excellent idea

Congratulations! You have just conducted a basic feasibility study for your new business idea. To complete your feasibility study, conduct a detailed investigation of the demand for your product or service. Go and find out from your potential customers exactly what they want and determine what factors that influence their buying decisions.

Then conduct a further analysis of your competition. You know who the competition is; how likely is it that your business will succeed? Can a small student business compete against established businesses in your market?

Try to forecast prospective sales. Will your business idea generate the financial returns that you need to survive?

Finally, look at your projected expenses. Will your projected sales support your planned expenses? When will your business break even? Read on; the chapters that follow will help you find the answers to all these questions and get your business up and running.

3

WHY STUDENTS SHOULD CONSIDER A FRANCHISE

Franchising is something every student entrepreneur should consider, though it may not be for everyone. Running a franchise is a good option for the student entrepreneur. Rather than struggling to establish your customer base, you capitalize on the franchise's experience and previous marketing efforts. However, a franchisor requires its owners/operators to fit into an existing framework and follow an established system. To be successful in a franchise you must work effectively as part of a team and be prepared to compromise some of your independence.

a. WHAT IS A FRANCHISE?

A franchise is a right granted by a company, the franchisor, to an individual or company, the franchisee, to use or sell the franchisor's ideas, goods, brands, or services under its name.

An ideal student franchise is a continuing and supportive relationship in which you, the franchisee, and the franchisor work together for mutual benefit.

In a well-established franchise, start-up risks are lowered considerably because problems such as underfunding and inexperience are avoided.

Reputable franchisors may offer you exclusive territories and support on a continuing basis.

b. ADVANTAGES AND DISADVANTAGES OF OWNING A FRANCHISE

1. Advantages

For students, advantages include the following:

(a) *Franchise reputation and recognition:* By signing on with a franchisor, you instantly take on its reputation and goodwill, and benefit from its prior advertising activities. Most franchisors have some sort of trademark or symbol that is well-known to the buying public and will be accepted readily.

(b) *Training and management assistance*: Most reputable franchisors provide some sort of training and management assistance for both the start-up of your business and long-term management. Usually this will be in the form of seminars, corporate guidebooks, and experienced advice. The franchisor usually has knowledge from operating many outlets and has developed a background of success.

(c) *Economies of scale in buying*: Most franchises are large enough so that its total buying power allows it to purchase goods and services at substantial discounts from what independent business owners pay. This dramatically decreases your operating costs.

(d) *Financial assistance*: Most franchisors can help you get loans or will structure its royalty payments to coincide with your high income periods. This helps free valuable cash for other profit-making expenses.

(e) *Promotional assistance*: All franchises do promotional work, both locally and nationally. This takes some of the burden of managing and creating promotions off your shoulders. As well, most franchisors assist its franchisees by creating specific advertising campaigns. Advertisements, fliers, posters, and contests are ready-made for you, as well as discounted distribution.

(f) *Limited risk*: Far fewer franchised businesses fail than independent businesses. The franchisor wants you to succeed and makes every effort to ensure that you do. The franchisor helps you prepare your business plan and works with you to generate customers.

A franchise needs you just as much as you need it; it's an arrangement designed for mutual benefit. A hard-working student franchisee offers these advantages to the franchisor:

(a) *Franchisee royalty payments*: You pay the franchisor a percentage of sales. The franchisor, in effect, receives an income from you.

(b) *Promotional assistance*: Your money and efforts, while purposely directed to promote your individual business, ultimately help the franchisor gain national acceptance and market share. This is much faster and easier in a franchise environment than in a sole-owner business.

(c) *Faster expansion and corporate recognition*: A franchisor can expand much more quickly through franchising and can gain national or international recognition by capitalizing on the motivation, financial resources, and local networking abilities of their franchises. This lets the franchisor cover a new market quickly and eliminate the possibility of competition entering and taking away part of the market.

(d) *Franchisee motivation*: As an independent business person, you are much more eager to see your business work and become profitable than a hired manager is who doesn't have a stake in the business.

(e) *Committed franchisee attention to detail*: You want your business to succeed and will do what it takes to do the job right and satisfy the customers. The franchisor gains since it is ultimately the franchise company whose reputation and goodwill is being built up.

2. Disadvantages

(a) *Royalty payments*: Royalty payments must be made to the franchisor; this means reduced profits and increased expenses for you. This can include a franchise fee, a percentage-based fee, advertising fees, and the costs of buying equipment and supplies. Sometimes your return for your royalty payments may be insignificant compared to the costs you have had to meet.

(b) *Limited creativity*: You must conform to the franchisor's standard operations. According to the contract, you must follow certain ways and means of marketing and selling specific products and services. You cannot start marketing a different product or service under the franchisor's name or use your franchise to do any business outside of the contract. Even if you have good ideas for new products or a different way of doing things, you must conform to the franchisor's stipulations.

(c) *Limited market area*: Franchisors limit your market area by specifying the area in which you are allowed to do business. However, this area may be too small or already over-saturated, and will seriously hamper your ability to produce business.

(d) *Limited independence*: Franchisors limit your independence in decision-making and control the products you sell, your business and record keeping procedures, and the area that you service.

(e) *Different priorities*: Franchisors and franchisees may have different priorities. Since franchisors have long-term perspectives and in most cases franchisees will be primarily interested in short-term profit, there may be conflict between quality and profit. The franchisor may insist on long-term, often one-sided legal commitments.

c. WHAT TO EXPECT FROM A FRANCHISOR AND WHAT IT EXPECTS FROM YOU

Some franchisors do virtually all the initial work of starting the new operation; others do very little. Some franchisors offer continuing support. This may include regular meetings and suggestions, monthly news communications, and local advertising. Some leave you with all of the responsibility and offer no help at all. If there are certain things that you expect from the franchisor, make sure they are written into the contract. You can be sure that the franchisor will do the same vis-à-vis its expectations of you.

In general, the expectations of the franchisee (you) often include payment of a royalty up front and/or a percentage of the gross sales. Royalties can range from around 12% to 24% of your gross income. Typically, good student franchises will not have an initial fee. There may, however, be fees for equipment or services that the franchisor provides before your business is up and running. As well, a franchisor usually expects its franchisees to sell only its products or services in an assigned territory.

In general, you can expect the franchisor to offer you a territory, specific products or services to sell, training on how to sell them, and the features of the market. It may offer help buying equipment and/or weekly consultations. However, a franchisor is not legally responsible for particulars that are not specifically stipulated in the contract, even if the franchisor says it will do it. Have everything put in writing; don't assume that the franchisor will take care of it.

Do not assume the franchise organization is your safety net; ultimately it is you who is responsible for seeing that your business succeeds. Make sure you know what you are paying for. Don't sign a franchise contract immediately; spend time getting it reviewed by others.

d. HOW TO IDENTIFY LOCAL FRANCHISE OPPORTUNITIES

Finding local franchise opportunities that are suitable for a student-run business is easy if you know where to look. Most student franchisors actively advertise on college and university campuses. The trick is to know where and when to look.

Students should usually start looking in the fall. This may seem early for a summer business; however, this ensures that there are good territories available and gives you time to evaluate your prospective franchisor. The best place to start your search is on the bulletin boards or public posting areas of your school library or social area.

In addition, it is also useful to contact your college or university career center since they are probably aware of which franchisors are advertising and where.

If these areas do not generate a suitable franchise opportunity, your Chamber of Commerce or local government agency that deals with summer business loans will have a good idea of which franchises have been run by local students in the past and how to get in touch with those franchisors.

Taking the time to search these franchisors out early can save you a lot of frustration and stress in the long run and ensure that you find a reputable franchisor to do business with.

e. HOW TO DECIDE ON THE RIGHT FRANCHISE

Investigate your prospective franchisor thoroughly. Consider the total fees charged, how long the franchisor has been in business, and how successful the franchise has been in previous years. What is the franchisor's current financial situation? Can it meet its advertising and supply demands? The franchisor might be unable to live up to the commitment in the franchising agreement. How many other franchises are there?

See if you can provide the same product or service without the franchisor. If so, maybe you don't need to be part of a franchise. Consider if the sales targets of the franchisor are realistic; have they been met in previous years? Unscrupulous franchisors might be selling franchises that have little merit and may try to dazzle you with big sales and profit figures. BEWARE!

Consider whether the market for your franchise product or service is open or saturated, declining or growing. All of these factors seriously affect your business profitability and dictate how much energy you have to spend on advertising and looking for new customers. As well,

remember that the franchises might already saturate the market in your area.

Ensure that the advantages outweigh the disadvantages. Look at inexperience, underfunding, and no proven track record as serious disadvantages. If the franchisor offers an established name or trademark that has public awareness and confidence, consider these advantages. Public opinion, current market saturation in your area, terms of contractual commitment, personal interests, and abilities will all affect your specific personal decision.

Finally, ask for the names and phone numbers of previous franchise owners in your area to get a good idea of what that franchisor is really like.

Table #1 helps you compare several prospective franchise opportunities to determine the best one.

Learn as much as you can about franchising before you make a commitment. In the United States, check with the International Franchise Association in Washington, D.C. In Canada, the Canadian Franchise Association provides information about franchising in Canada. While these two organizations are accessible and friendly, they cannot give information about specific student-run franchises. They do, however, offer great advice on how to select a franchise and they have booklets on the laws and regulations of franchising which can be very helpful in evaluating, researching general problems, and deciding on a franchise opportunity. Write to:

International Franchise Association
900 - 1350 New York Avenue
Washington, D.C. 20005
Tel: (202) 628-8000

Canadian Franchise Association
5045 Orbitor Drive
Building 12, Unit 1
Mississauga, Ontario L4W 4Y4
Tel: (905) 625-2896 or 1-800-665-4232

TABLE #1
COMPARING FRANCHISE OPPORTUNITIES

FEATURES	AN EXAMPLE OF A GOOD FRANCHISE	YOUR POSSIBLE FRANCHISE OPPORTUNITIES		
		1	2	3
Franchise name:	We Love Students Co.			
1. Franchise fee:	$ Nil			
2. Contract length, restrictions:	Summer term or one operating year			
3. Training offered:	Yes; also management, organization, and set-up			
4. Royalty fees:	3% to 24%, depending on marketing			
5. Ongoing supervision and training:	Weekly evaluation call-ins and help sessions			
6. Number of franchises currently in operation:	Franchise should be at least province-/state-wide; the bigger the better — no less than 50 franchises			
7. Age of franchisor:	At least five years old; can supply pro forma for franchises each year			
8. Estimated income:	Not less than $3,000; preferably look for one that can match or exceed your required income for the summer			
9. Bankers', accountants', and lawyers' opinions:	Acceptable idea and well-defined contract, affordable with realistic sales goals			
10. Other conditions:	Advice in choosing equipment, location, ongoing consultation			

f. LEGAL CONSIDERATIONS AND PITFALLS

The most common problem facing franchisees is that the franchise may not meet the expected profit level. Don't have unrealistic expectations of your business and don't let others convince you that your company can meet unrealistic sales goals.

Read your franchise agreement carefully and consult a lawyer before you sign it. You should be fully aware of your commitments to the franchisor financially, and in terms of management and time. Be confident that both sides can meet those commitments.

Keep in mind that as a franchisee you are legally required to make payments to the franchise whether your franchise makes money or not. These payments can include a franchise fee, a percentage-based royalty fee, advertising fees, and the costs of buying equipment and supplies. Be sure you are comfortable with making these payments and can make them even if your business does not reach its sales goals. Otherwise you may find yourself having to deal with legal problems that take time and can be very frustrating.

The best way to avoid all these problems is to ask questions, research your potential franchises's background using the library and Better Business Bureau, and talk with previous franchisees and franchise customers. Remember, see a lawyer before you sign!

CASE STUDY

College Pro Painters franchise

College Pro Painters Limited (College Pro) is a student franchise in the residential painting industry. It represents an excellent opportunity for first-time and intermediate entrepreneurs who want to run a profitable business and gain business know-how from first-hand experience.

College Pro has grown steadily for over 25 years and has shown stability and commitment to its values. In fact, thanks to the company's consistent effort and unique emphasis on demographic marketing, studies show that 80% to 90% of College Pro's target market know about it. Each year across the United States and Canada, College Pro provides extensive training and management support to almost 800 college and university students.

For a minimal deposit and monthly royalty payments, student entrepreneurs are given an exclusive territory. All new franchisees are trained and given ongoing field assistance in a number of business management skills including goal setting, business planning, financial and managerial accounting and budgeting, time management, and scheduling.

Since the franchisee's leadership skills will be essential in managing employees and selling, all franchisees are also given training in selling, production management, conflict management, and delegation skills. For those who are not familiar with the painting industry, College Pro provides training in paint systems, estimating, and general painting techniques.

The company also helps the franchisee deal with the legal and safety issues of running a business by offering training and ongoing support on issues such as job safety, payroll, and government requirements. Through College Pro, franchisees can offer customers a two-year guarantee against paint failure and the reassurance of $5 million in liability insurance.

The economies of scale provided by College Pro allow managers to secure discounts and lines of credit with major paint and related equipment suppliers. There are substantial discounts on crew and painter kits, signs, and advertising materials. Its system of training and ongoing support has proven for many years to be both profitable and educational.

4
BUSINESS ARRANGEMENTS

a. YOUR BUSINESS STRUCTURE

Every business is a legal entity and has a legal structure. Businesses take one of three forms: a sole proprietorship, a partnership, or a corporation. As a student business owner, you will probably be a sole proprietor, because this is the easiest to operate and cheapest to register.

However, it is smart to be aware of all the options since there are many different business possibilities out there. This chapter outlines the advantages and disadvantages, how to register, and the costs associated with each.

1. Sole proprietorship

A sole proprietorship is a business owned and managed by one person. This is the situation in which a student can say, "this business is mine." The sole proprietorship is the oldest and most common form of legal business ownership. In Canada and the United States most sole proprietorships are service-based businesses.

The major advantages of being a sole proprietor are the following:

(a) *Easy start-up:* You only need to register your name and get any licenses or permits necessary for your type of business. Other than that, you can start doing business right away.

(b) *All profits are yours:* You are the only owner of the business and so are entitled to all the profits from that business.

(c) *Taxed just like normal personal income:* The business is taxed as part of your personal income, so completing your income tax return is far less complicated than for a corporation.

(d) *Easy to close business:* If you want to end your business all you have to do is cancel your licenses and permits and stop doing business.

(e) *Great flexibility in decision making:* You are the sole owner and therefore make all the decisions.

(f) *Personal rewards from independent achievement:* As a sole proprietorship the business is truly yours. You can take the credit for making it work.

The major disadvantages of forming a sole proprietorship are the following:

(a) *Personal risk for business liabilities:* You are fully liable for any business debts, even if they extend beyond the business assets.

(b) *No help in finding start-up funds:* You must raise funds on your own, with only your personal credit history to support you.

(c) *All decisions must be made independently:* Ultimately, you must make all the business decisions on your own. Right or wrong, you have sole responsibility for the outcome of everything your company does.

2. Partnership

If you are hoping to start a business with a friend, relative, or other person it will be necessary to start a partnership. A partnership is established when two of more individuals agree to combine their financial, managerial, and technical abilities for the purpose of operating a company for profit.

A partnership offers the following advantages:

(a) *Easy start-up:* Registering as a partnership is similar to setting up as a sole proprietorship except that you must complete a partnership agreement.

(b) *Help in making decisions:* There is more cash available for investment since there are more people involved.

(c) *Help in raising funds:* Getting credit is easier since the credit history of all partners can be used to secure funds.

(d) *Pooled education and experience:* A partnership offers more opportunity for specialization than a sole proprietorship because you can combine various people's experience and education.

(e) *Personal rewards from independent achievement:* Although in a partnership you have to share decisions, you still form a major part of discussions and the end result of the business is up to you.

(f) *Taxed just like normal personal income:* Like a sole proprietorship, your partnership income can be entered as part of your personal income. No further income tax forms are required.

The disadvantages of a partnership are the following:

(a) *Personal risk for business liabilities:* Like a sole proprietorship, a partnership is liable above and beyond the partners' investment in the business.

(b) *Risk of incompatible views and opinions:* Having a partnership requires that you be able to communicate and interact well with your partner or partners. Disagreements can seriously slow down decisions and hamper business progress. Skills are needed to bring all partners' views together. For first-time student entrepreneurs, starting a business while maintaining profits and friendship among partners can be difficult.

(c) *Locked into business:* Since you are not the only decision maker, your investment is frozen in the business unless both partners agree to close the business or buy the other partner out. This makes it much more difficult to leave a business if you are not enjoying it or if the return is not what you had expected.

(d) *Less flexibility in decision making (than a sole proprietorship):* The decisions must be made by all partners. Your opinions and ideas must be approved by the partners before they can be acted upon.

Keep in mind that if you decide to start a partnership, you must have a partnership agreement. A partnership agreement usually states the name, location, the nature of the business, the names of the partners, as well as each partners' contribution in terms of money, skills, and participation in managing the business. The duties of each partner, how the profits and losses will be shared, and the procedure for withdrawal of one or more partners must also be stated in this agreement.

Having such an agreement may seem unnecessary for a student business, but it can be very useful in providing a clear understanding of expectations in case difficulties arise.

3. Corporation

A corporation can be defined as a business organization that exists as a separate legal entity from its owners. This book does not go into detail here because corporations are technically difficult and costly to start. They are best suited to long-term or full-time businesses and students should think carefully before considering this form of business ownership for their part-time or seasonal business.

A corporation offers business owners the following advantages:

(a) *It is its own legal entity:* The business exists regardless and independent of the owner. It is taxed separately from your personal income tax.

(b) *No personal risk for business liabilities:* You cannot be held personally liable for debts if your company does not succeed. You are only committed to the extent of your investment.

(c) *Business exists separate from owner:* Since the business is a separate legal entity, it can exist indefinitely, or until its registration expires.

(d) *Easy to buy and sell:* A corporation can be bought or sold simply by buying the shares of that company.

(e) *Greater ability to raise funds:* A corporation can sell shares to anybody, in any amount they choose. This allows for a greater ability to raise capital for the business set-up and expansion.

The disadvantages of choosing to operate as a corporation include the following:

(a) *Complicated double taxation:* There are special taxation laws for corporations that usually require detailed record keeping and assistance from an accountant.

(b) *More expensive set-up required:* The fees and procedures for setting up a corporation vary. However, registering as a corporation takes time, planning, and money; things that may be in short supply for the student entrepreneur who wants to get up and running.

(c) *Considerable government regulation and reporting laws:* Depending on your province or state, there are many more documents and annual updates that a corporation must file. Corporations come under much stricter control than sole proprietorships.

(d) *Division and restriction of leadership:* If the corporation is owned by several people, this can slow down decision making and decrease your company's competitiveness.

Table #2 summarizes the various types of business structures and their characteristics. Though you may start out as a sole proprietor, as your business grows, you may want to change your structure to add a new partner or create a limited corporation.

b. PART-TIME OR SEASONAL BUSINESS

1. The part-time business

A year-round, part-time business is a good idea if you have a service or product in demand all year. But you have to balance school and business. If you are in an academic program that is very demanding, it might be a good idea to scale things down during school or delegate the daily management to a trusted employee.

The biggest benefit of an all-year, part-time business is that you can keep your product or service in the market all the time. This makes your business more profitable and means that you don't need to continually reestablish your market every year like a summer business.

In addition, this type of business also lends itself well to expansion after graduation. Since you will have made solid contacts and developed a professional reputation, you will probably find it easy to expand your part-time business into a full-time career.

Finally, it is much easier to establish credit from both suppliers and banks if you are in operation all year, since you will

TABLE #2
COMPARISON OF BUSINESS STRUCTURES

Characteristic	Sole proprietorship	Partnership	Corporation
Ease and cost of set-up	Easy and low cost	Moderately difficult and low cost	Complicated and very costly
Ease and cost of dissolution	Easy and low cost	Moderately difficult and low cost	Complicated and very costly
Legal restrictions	Very few	Very few	Many
Personal liability for business debts	Owner is completely liable	Owner is liable to the extent of ownership	None
Availability of cash	Personal or loans	Personal, loans, or partner	Many avenues for acquiring capital
Tax rate and income reporting	Easy	Moderately easy	Difficult; special corporate tax forms
Number of owners	One	Two or more	One or more

30

have a more stable bank account, higher income, and, in general, a more reputable position.

Most students have to, or should, make their businesses secondary to school. With good time management and by delegating authority to employees, you can successfully manage a part-time business all year and go to school at the same time.

2. A seasonal business

As a student, you are free to pursue many different businesses. A good idea in any business is to start something you are interested in or that can eventually be expanded into a career. However, if you have a particularly profitable idea that may not be career-oriented for you, there is no harm in pursuing it in a short-term business such as a seasonal student business.

The advantage of a seasonal business is that if you don't like your business type or have become bored with it, you can simply start something else next year. Seasonal businesses still require you to spend the time analyzing an idea, researching the market, and creating a customer base every year.

Start to plan your seasonal business at least two to three months before you want to start selling your product or service. This is important since it will probably take you that long to go through the research, get set up, and build your customer base.

As well, a seasonal business requires you to do some accounting and follow-up work after the season is over. So you should be able to dedicate at least three or four days a month or so after your business has shut down.

In general, a seasonal business is a great way to explore different interests and career ideas or even just to make some money at an idea you know will be particularly profitable. However, you have to be prepared to do a lot of set-up and shutdown work every season.

3. Keeping your summer business alive after your first summer

Whether you want to run your summer business part-time or ensure that you can start it again the next summer, there are several things you can do to help keep your business alive over the inactive period.

First, at the end of the summer, make a list of people you did not do work for but who were very interested in your business. Chances are that next year, or in a few months, they will be ready to have the work done. If you remember to contact them again, they will probably contract you to do the work rather than a competitor.

Second, make a list of people you did work for. Contact as many of them as you can and make sure they are happy with everything. While you are on the phone, ask them if there is anything else they are considering having done, or if they know anyone that could use your service. Keep track of all the information you get from these people and remember to contact them as soon as possible or in the spring of next year. This way, you can assure yourself of having at least some work right from day one of your next year. After all, you have probably spent a great deal of time and money on advertising to find these customers; why not get as much from your current customers as possible?

Third, since it can be difficult to keep your summer business going during school, especially if you have a busy timetable, try to delegate some of the daily work to others. This is the only sane way to get the most out of both your education and your business. Try to schedule major business activities at times when school is not too demanding (i.e., on weekends and semester breaks). For more ideas about managing work time and school time, see chapter 16.

Finally, the best thing you can do for your business is to keep in touch with your suppliers and customers; let them know what is going on so they don't get the impression that you've gone out of business. Don't make commitments you can't keep in school or business. Having to cancel commitments, push them back, or doing rush jobs hurts your business in the long run and may damage your academic record or business reputation.

5
SETTING UP YOUR BUSINESS

a. CHOOSING A NAME

For your customers, your business name *is* the business. Over time, customers will know you and your reputation for quality service and reliability, but without a name that properly represents your business they may never call you in the first place. Your name is the first thing a potential customer sees and if it doesn't grab his or her attention right away you have probably lost that customer.

Choose a name that reflects your business; it should describe your service or product, or highlight some other special quality. What features of your business do you want people to pay attention to? Often, emphasizing factors such as quality, service, or reliability is a good idea in a student-run business. Many customers will be concerned that you are not a true professional in your particular field or that you are only doing this for quick cash and are not really concerned about quality.

Conversely, some customers jump at the chance to support a student entrepreneurial activity, so placing "student" in your name can be a good idea. However, if someday you decide to run this business full-time, you may want to change your business name. This will not only cost you another registration fee, but also the goodwill you may have built up while being a student. You can always let them know about your student status after they have gotten a chance to get to know you. Generally it is a good idea to leave "student" out of the name.

To give you a better idea of what makes for a good or bad business name, some sample names, with their benefits and drawbacks, have been included in Table #3.

Your name should represent the business you are in and shouldn't limit your business's range of activity. It should be pronounceable, memorable, and catchy.

b. HOW TO REGISTER YOUR BUSINESS

If the name of your business is different than your personal name you need to register it. For example, if John Student conducts his business as John Student he does not need to register the name. However, if he conducts his business as John Student Enterprises or JS Painting, he does need to register it.

In the United States, your city or county clerk will register your business name and can tell you if it is already in use.

In Canada, you can register your business name with the provincial companies branch. They can also tell you if the name is already in use by another business. The processing fee is usually around $60.

Try to gather as much information as possible on the following topics before you decide to register and start your business:

(a) Government rules and regulations

    (i) Licenses and permits

    (ii) Zoning and bylaw approval

    (iii) Federal, state/provincial, and municipal business taxes

    (iv) Sales tax and, in Canada, GST

TABLE #3
SAMPLE BUSINESS NAMES: BENEFITS AND DRAWBACKS

☺ **GOOD**   ☺ **OK (Warning)**   ☹ **BAD**

☺ **Student Quality Painters:** This name says what the business does, is easy to say, and is catchy. However, you must be sure you never intend to run this business as a career or that your customers won't worry about students doing the work, because the word "student" is in the company name.

☺ **Fun Time Boat Rentals:** This name is catchy, memorable, and clearly states what the business does. It limits the business only to a general field and suggests a reputable, professional, and fun business.

☺ **John Smith Consulting Services:** This name is rather general but does state what the business does. Since the owner's name is associated with the business name, if John Smith ever wants to sell his business, he will lose the goodwill associated with it.

☺ **ABC Window Cleaning:** This name gives the business type, but "ABC" does not lend any professionalism or personality to the business. It is, however, memorable and easy to say.

☺ **The Software People:** This is a memorable name and states what the business does. It is also catchy, but not very personal or interesting.

☹ **JD Works:** This name does not state what the business is associated with. Although it limits the business type very little, it does not make for a memorable or catchy name and customers are likely to overlook it for a more specific or professional business.

☹ **Second Choice Kitchens:** Who wants to buy something from a second choice kitchen? This name is catchy and memorable, but it has negative connotations and would probably be passed over for a company with a more reputable business name.

(v) Mandatory employment deductions

(vi) Labor laws

(vii) Consumer protection legislation

(viii) Quality controls

(b) Government or private sector assistance programs

   (i) For students

(ii) For entrepreneurs

(iii) For small businesses

(c) Regulations surrounding home-based businesses

   (i) Zoning and bylaws

   (ii) Tax implications and benefits

   (iii) Liability

(d) Any area in which you have little knowledge or experience

Knowing about any legal requirements in advance helps you to recognize potential business problems and opportunities before you have spent time and money on business registration. They can also help you decide on business structure, names, and market areas.

c. SETTING UP YOUR BUSINESS ADDRESS AND OFFICE

In order to have a professional business, you will need a place of operation, a contact address, and a telephone. A student business must meet all the local registration, zoning, and bylaws that apply to all businesses.

Your business is required by law to have a chief place of business. To your customers and the government this is represented by your mailing address. Keep in mind that the type of business will influence whether you want to use your home address, a post office box number, or rent or borrow space from someone else. Consider whether you need customers to come to your business or whether you can go to them.

1. Office in your home

Most student entrepreneurs want to run their business from their home. This is the most cost-effective thing to do and it is usually sufficient. Generally, a separate phone line, a large table for books and accounting records, and perhaps a computer and fax machine can be set up somewhere at home. Depending on the type of business you have, the home office may work just fine. Having business meetings outside your office allows you to easily maintain a home office, without sacrificing professionalism.

The main concern is that in some areas there will be bylaws and zoning laws limiting business activities with high traffic volume or manufacturing in residential areas. You should make sure that no such laws prohibit your business before you start working from home.

Ultimately, the best mailing address for a student business is your chief place of residence. This way, your location costs you nothing and if you are successful and run the business over several years, your customers will know where to find you.

2. Office outside your home

New student entrepreneurs should avoid having an office outside the home, at least until you are sure that your business idea is going to work. Renting an office is a large expense. On the other hand, if you can find someone willing to rent to you on a short-term basis or who will let you borrow the space, then this is not a bad idea.

d. TELEPHONE LINE

1. Using your current home phone

Unless you are in a business in which your customers are unlikely to have to call you, it is not a very good idea to use your home phone as your business phone. It is not very business-like or professional to just answer the phone with "hello" or have another family member answer the phone and have to yell to get you. Also, in some areas, having a separate business line is a legal requirement of running a business.

2. A separate phone at home

Try to set up a separate phone line if you are working from home. This allows you to answer the phone with "(Your Business Name), how can I help you," or something similar. This lends a professional tone and a certain sense of permanence to your business that often helps customers feel more secure about doing business with you. Again, it may be a legal requirement to install a separate business line.

3. Answering machine and service

You should try to have an answering machine always on if you are out. Customers may call on a spur-of-the-moment basis and if you don't answer that call they may never call back. Leave a message like: "Thank you for calling (business name). We're sorry we are unable to take your call at the moment, but your call is important to us. Please leave a detailed message at the tone and we will return your call as soon as possible. Thank you!"

It is a good idea to have call waiting or a similar feature installed on the line in case customers call while you are on the phone. There is nothing more frustrating for customers than getting a busy signal when they are trying to get you to come and do some work for them.

4. Discounted long distance rates

Many local companies offer discounts on long distance service. Since you will probably be making many calls, it is not a bad idea to sign on with one that you feel is reputable. In the long run this may add up to major savings.

Remember, every customer is potential business and you want to talk to as many as possible. The best way to do this is to make yourself as accessible as possible.

e. BUSINESS BANKING

As a student entrepreneur you will probably be looking for a bank that can offer you many different services. One bank alone may not offer you all the services you are looking for, but you should expect certain basic ones.

Ask your bank about the products and services they offer small business clients. Find out which banks specifically support small business. All banks are not alike and they may have different services and policies so shopping around is a good idea. Ultimately, you should try to deal with only one account manager. Start by setting up a business deposit and checking account in the name of your business. This will allow you to cash checks made out to your business and pay suppliers and employees by check.

Typically most banks will charge around 60¢ per transaction in a business account. If you need loans for your business, different banks have different loan schemes for student entrepreneurs. It pays to shop around.

Ensure that you have a good relationship with your bank. This will help to make sure that your requests are met properly, quickly, and conveniently. To do this, make your banker part of your team. Let him or her know what you are looking for and why. If you are clear, thorough, and realistic, your bank will be able to recommend proper solutions to you.

1. Deposit accounts

Most banks offer some type of current account. This is the very minimum you need for your business banking. This account typically features a checking account for which you receive monthly statements. Sometimes you might receive interest on your business balance.

2. Packages

Many small business clients opt for a pre-arranged package of options that may be set up to handle cash, process checks, do payroll, take deposits, and give loans. This type of package is a good idea if your bank is offering it at a cost-effective price. It can save you time by allowing you to do all your banking transactions at one time and in one bank. Remember, time is worth money too.

f. INSURANCE

It is very important that you discuss your particular insurance needs with a professional. A student entrepreneur may not need any insurance at all, but it is important that you be aware of your risks and evaluate which ones could, or should, be covered by insurance.

Some franchises offer insurance as part of their royalty payments. Often these types of plans are more comprehensive and less expensive than an individual business owner could get on his or her own.

1. Purpose of insurance

The major purpose of insurance is to minimize the risk of interrupting operations or losing profit. Insurance decreases risk by minimizing and absorbing the repercussions resulting from accidents and liability in general. Insurance does not actually decrease the probability of an accident from happening and should not be used to justify unsafe work practices or inefficient operations.

Every student entrepreneur should take every means possible to decrease the necessity of insurance and always purchase insurance when necessary. Saving a few hundred dollars now may seem like a great idea. However, accidents without insurance can cost you far more than $100, not to mention lost time and unneeded stress.

Also, since in many areas the responsibility of accidents ultimately falls on the property owner, having insurance can often be a selling point and help customers feel more comfortable about doing business with you. It is important to investigate the proper insurance coverage for your business. Most often student businesses do not need any special insurance, but be aware of any law stating that your particular business must be insured.

Sometimes banks require insurance if you are taking out a loan to finance your venture, so it is also a good idea to find out what your bank representative has to say regarding insurance.

2. What to look for when buying insurance

In general, when the possibility of a large loss is great, consider buying insurance. Look for companies that can insure you on a monthly basis. Signing long insurance contracts is not necessary and you can save money by concentrating your insurance when it is really needed. Sometimes companies will even insure individual jobs.

3. Types of insurance

Before you can do anything about insuring the risks your business faces, you must first be aware of what they are. As you review the different types of insurance in the list below, consider whether your business could possibly be subject to any of them. Note any you think might pose a high risk for your business; make sure to ask your insurance broker about them. There are four major types of insurance a student should consider:

(a) *Personal or disability:* Personal insurance is to help recoup lost profits due to injury or disability. Since students must earn enough during the summer to recover their investment and pay for school, this type of insurance is one to be considered.

(b) *Employee:* Most of your employee insurance needs will be covered by state or provincial workers' compensation insurance that all employers must pay, based on a percentage of employee income. However, if a worker gets sick, will your business cover the cost of their absence?

(c) *Equipment or vehicle:* All vehicles must be insured. However, if a vehicle is used specifically for business it may require special insurance coverage. Be sure you have insurance that meets government requirements. Also, depending on your vehicle's value and usefulness, you may want to consider collision, theft, or damage insurance as well.

(d) *Damages:* These types of insurance needs get more specific depending on the type of business. Consider the likelihood of someone wanting to sue you. A home-based business will probably not be covered under your home insurance. Since injuries and damages are ultimately the property owner's problem, having insurance that frees them of this is often a selling point that will help customers feel more comfortable about you doing the job.

(e) *Bank loan insurance:* Many financial institutions offer business loan insurance plans that help cover missed payments of interests in the event of difficulties or unforeseen tragedies.

Remember, the main purpose of insurance is to control risk. Talk to a qualified insurance broker about the kind and amount of insurance you need, if any. Consider the enormity of risks and the practicality of insuring them, but don't be oversold.

g. OTHER LEGALITIES

Seek legal advice when possible. You may think this is expensive, but many lawyers will offer free, short-term advice. And if you let them know you are a student, they may be willing to offer complimentary help beyond the initial consultation.

Be very cautious of signing contracts with suppliers, franchisors, contractors, or others. These are legal commitments and unless you fully understand them and are capable of meeting their specifications, do not sign them. Remember, ask questions about anything you are confused or concerned about.

If you are writing contracts with customers, a template copy should be reviewed by a lawyer to ensure it is legally binding. It should state the work you will do, when you will do it, at what price, terms of payment, and who will provide all the goods and services.

Student businesses are often eligible for free or low-cost legal advice from a provincial or state legal aid plan usually located at a student legal aid services office on campus. They have law students who are supervised by a lawyer.

Consider whether you need a license or permit to operate your business. Often licenses and permits are used to control businesses that pose special problems regarding health, fire, food, or government laws, and they protect the public in general. Your local government small business service center will have more information.

6
YOUR BUSINESS PLAN

a. CREATING A BUSINESS PLAN

A student entrepreneur who wants to be successful should start his or her business with a solid plan. A business plan serves as your guide to getting where you want to be. Think of it as a resume; it requires a little more thought and time up front, but is well worth it in the end.

Your business plan serves two major purposes:

(a) It helps you to clarify your goals and focus on defining every detail of your business opportunity. Your plan should serve as a measuring tool to set objectives and the time frame in which to attain them.

(b) It is a must if you want to apply for any type of financing for your business.

Checklist #1 lists all the items you need to include in your business plan.

b. EXPECTATIONS

When you are setting goals and getting started, consider the external environment and the effect it will have on your business expectations. By looking at other products or services in your market and talking to potential customers, you should be able to form realistic expectations regarding sales and expenses as well as establish a realistic equilibrium point, or break-even point.

Then you should decide if those break-even and profit points are sufficient for your income and profit needs. If they are not, you may have some success at changing them by reorganizing your business plan and finding more efficient ways to lower your expenses. However, don't expect that you will be able to change your break-even point dramatically. If it is too high, the only way to lower it is to change what you are doing. Simply doing more work is usually not sufficient to increase profitability in a student-run business.

As you gain experience, try to draw on what you have learned. Try to understand what caused you to miss certain expectations, as well as what you did to meet others. This will help you set better expectations in the future.

As a rule of thumb, you should always set your expectations with sales at a predicted minimum and expenses at their predicted maximum when completing your business plan. This way the chances of meeting your goal are much greater, even if you have underestimated expenses or overestimated sales. If you find that setting your expectations this way does not allow your business to make sufficient profit, then you should find ways to limit your expenses or ensure that you can attain higher sales goals. In the long run, by setting your expectations this way, you will find business profitable and be able to establish reasonable expectations.

c. DEVELOPING A TIMELINE

What your goals are and how to meet those goals has now been set out in the business plan. (In chapter 7, Worksheet #8, your cash flow forecast can also help you assess your company's financial needs and goals.)

CHECKLIST #1
ITEMS IN A BUSINESS PLAN

1. Business information

- ☐ Business address
- ☐ Business phone number
- ☐ Names of people involved in the business, including their addresses and phone numbers
- ☐ A statement of business structure, e.g., sole proprietorship, partnership, or corporation
- ☐ A list of any necessary permits or licenses required to do business
- ☐ The participants' social insurance/security numbers
- ☐ Name of your bank and, if applicable, insurance agent

2. The purpose of your business

- ☐ Outline your objectives for the business
- ☐ Estimate required start-up funds and where the money will come from
- ☐ Explain how you are going to repay the funds, if necessary
- ☐ Describe your experience and skills and how they can help you in this business

3. Management

- ☐ Who will run the business
- ☐ Your expected income and necessary owner drawings, when, and how much

4. Operating location

- ☐ Why you chose your location
- ☐ Aspects of your location that benefit your business
- ☐ Disadvantages to your chosen location

5. Personnel

- ☐ Staff you will need to hire now, or in the future
- ☐ Who will train the staff
- ☐ How you will set pay rates and what incentives will you use to promote efficiency

6. Suppliers
- ☐ Who your suppliers are
- ☐ What they will supply
- ☐ Will you get credit from your suppliers?
- ☐ Will you be renting anything, and if so, from whom?

7. Your market
- ☐ Who your customers are
- ☐ Whether there is growth in your market
- ☐ How you will advertise and promote your business
- ☐ What niche you hope to fill

8. Competition
- ☐ Who your competition is
- ☐ Why the customers should do business with you instead of a competitor

9. Financial information
- ☐ A projection of your cash flow, income, and expenses
- ☐ A balance sheet to understand the funds you have and their availability
- ☐ The equipment and other major supplies required with their costs

A timeline helps you reach those goals by assigning a date and time that you expect to reach each goal. Student business timelines are sufficient if they include:

(a) a daily to-do list,

(b) a weekly priorities list,

(c) a monthly objectives list, and

(d) a list of how missed goals will be reviewed and completed.

d. SETTING GOALS AND REVISING THE BUSINESS PLAN TO MEET YOUR GOALS

Use your business plan to set goals. If by the end of a predetermined time frame, say one month, you are not on target, revise your business plan and carefully analyze what went wrong. You can then adjust your goals with a new understanding of how to achieve them.

When setting your goals, it is important to maintain a balanced life; don't let your business monopolize your time so that the things you like about your business become the things you hate. Keep on top of this by being aware of the effect your business is having on you and those around you. If you don't like where things are going, make changes, delegate responsibility, or reconsider your business's direction.

Worksheet #7 helps you set goals realistically and proactively.

WORKSHEET #7
GOAL SETTING

This year (or summer) my goal is:

   1. To earn $_____

   2. To work _____ hours per week.

   3. To take _____ days of vacation.

   4. In my personal life, I will (a) _____

                                    (b) _____

                                    (c) _____

FILL OUT A SECTION FOR EACH WEEK OF BUSINESS OPERATION*

To accomplish my goals:

My Week One objectives are: 1. _____

                                      2. _____

                                      3. _____

        Accomplished?   YES___   NO___

My Week Two objectives are: 1. _____

                                        2. _____

                                      3. _____

        Accomplished?   YES___   NO___

My Week Three objectives are: 1. _____

                                        2. _____

                                      3. _____

        Accomplished?   YES___   NO___

My Week Four objectives are: 1. _____

                                        2. _____

                                      3. _____

        Accomplished?   YES___   NO___

* Note: These should be specific expectations. Week One should be devoted to business planning and should be started six to eight weeks before you intend to begin doing business.

FILL OUT FOR EACH MONTH OF BUSINESS OPERATIONS*

My Month One objectives are: 1. _____

2. _____

3. _____

4. _____

Accomplished?   YES___   NO___

My Month Two objectives are: 1. _____

2. _____

3. _____

4. _____

Accomplished?   YES___   NO___

My Month Three objectives are: 1. _____

2. _____

3. _____

4. _____

Accomplished?   YES___   NO___

My Month Four objectives are: 1. _____

2. _____

3. _____

4. _____

Accomplished?   YES___   NO___

*Note: These should be general goals and expectations. Month One begins the day you start doing business. The last month should end one month after your business has closed. It concerns the wrap-up of sales and production, final accounting, and any shutdown procedures needed. If you intend to run your business the following year, spend some of this time organizing your business for next year's start-up.

7
FINANCING YOUR IDEA

Finding start-up funds can often be the most frustrating part of starting a new student business. Start planning early. Since most students have limited funds and limited personal income, they often have to rely on outside sources for most of the money. In order to get outside funding, students have to analyze exactly how much money is needed, for what, and when. The first step is to analyze what your expenses will be for your particular business and determine just how much money you need.

a. COSTS OF STARTING YOUR OWN BUSINESS

Unlike a conventional job, starting your own business will originally start out costing you money. Student entrepreneurs should recognize that it is their responsibility to obtain the necessary supplies and equipment at reasonable prices. They must also find those with the highest quality. These will make up the largest amount of their fixed costs, thus determining how fast they can make back their investment and start making a profit. A typical student business will have the following start-up costs.

1. Business registration

(a) *Registration:* Registering your business is required by some industries to ensure that only reputable and educated professionals are in business. As well, if you plan to operate under a name other than your own, you will be required to register your business.

(b) *Licenses:* Certain products, such as liquor, can only be sold under special license.

(c) *Permits:* Certain businesses, such as street vendors, are required to have a vendor's permit for public security and tax collection. Food sales require special health permits to ensure that all health standards are met.

2. Office supplies

(a) *Stationery:* Stationery is necessary to give your business a professional look.

(b) *Business cards:* Business cards lend security and professionalism to a business. They are also a quick and easy way to get your name out to prospective customers and suppliers.

(c) *Forms for record keeping and invoicing:* These are required to help you meet your legal accounting requirements. As well, they help you stay organized, manage finances, and present a professional appearance.

3. Office equipment

(a) *Computer:* A computer can be very useful in managing customer and supplier names, handling finances, and producing professional communications such as letters, estimates, and the like.

(b) *Fax machine:* More and more, fax machines are becoming important to the student entrepreneur. They help you get information quickly from suppliers and customers and help you distribute information quickly and efficiently.

4. Insurance

There are a variety of insurance plans available for small businesses. Most commonly, a student business will be interested in either personal, employee, damages, or equipment and/or property insurance. It is best to talk to an insurance representative about what insurable risks are associated with your particular business before you start selling your product or service. Your business may or may not require any insurance, but it is important to be aware of the laws and risks that affect you and what you can do about it. See chapter 6 for a detailed discussion on insurance.

5. Equipment

(a) Used vs. new

The decision to buy new or used should be based on how much a piece of equipment is damaged by its use. Obviously if a ladder has been used responsibly 1,000 times, it can be counted on to work 1,000 times more. The same cannot be said for a lawn mower or other mechanical devices.

Buying used is a good way to get equipment and save valuable cash reserves. Most of the value of a piece of equipment is lost in the first-time purchase. If you decide to buy used, you can probably sell that equipment for 80% to 100% of what you paid for it. If you decide to buy new, you may lose as much as 50% in the first year of use alone. You need to weigh the benefits of up-front cash savings against the possibility of breakdown and repair or replacement.

(b) Rental

Student businesses should consider renting equipment only if it is very expensive to buy or if it is infrequently used. If you will be needing a piece of equipment frequently it will eventually cost you much less to buy it than to continue renting it.

This idea, however, makes the assumption that your business will be successful and create jobs in which to use the equipment. If you are concerned that the cost of large up-front purchases of equipment may not be returned by your business, then renting equipment until you are sure your business will work can also be a good idea. If you need specialty equipment or equipment that could be difficult to resell if your business is shut down or fails, then renting is again a good idea.

6. Vehicle

Almost all student businesses require a vehicle. This can be the largest expense associated with the start-up costs. Remember that in the beginning, most student businesses will not require the purchase of a vehicle for business purposes only. Borrowing a vehicle when needed can often be sufficient, as long as you take care of the vehicle so that you can be assured of using it on a reliable basis.

If you are sure you will require a vehicle regularly and are confident that your business will succeed, there is also the option of buying a used vehicle. Whichever way you chose, make sure that the vehicle is reliable and will be as cost-effective as possible.

Also, when considering vehicle expenses, remember that maintenance and gas are also required to run a vehicle. These variable expenses can be significant and should not be overlooked.

7. Miscellaneous

There are always miscellaneous expenses associated with starting a business. If you have done a good job of planning out your expenses then this type of expense should only be a relatively small percentage of the total start-up costs. However, since no one is perfect and not everything can be anticipated, you should always include a small amount for miscellaneous expenses in your business start-up planning.

Sample #1 shows average start-up costs based on typical student businesses.

Now that you have some idea of the expenses associated with your business, try to calculate the amount of sales needed for your business to begin to break-even. The break-even point represents the point where your total costs and total income are equal. Breaking even depends on your fixed costs (e.g., office supplies, insurance, and essential equipment), variable costs (employee wages, suppliers, and materials), and the price you can charge for your product or service.

Your break-even point must be a realistic figure. The lower it is, the faster you can start making a profit. Try to work out your break-even point before you start doing business so you know the impact of any decisions you may make. Deciding to give discounts, raising employee wages, or buying extra supplies all affect your profitability.

Finally, remember that when you make cost predictions it is always best to overestimate costs and underestimate sales. In general, be conservative. This way, if, for some reason, unforeseen difficulties come up, as they always do, you have a cushion to fall back on.

b. HOW MUCH MONEY IS NEEDED?

Try to start a business that is as affordable as possible. If starting your business means that you have to borrow a large sum of money, then that business may not be for you. Remember, you want to minimize your chances of losing money. Many students need to borrow at least some funds. Start small and expand as funds become available. Don't start a business with too high a commitment to outside financing. In case the business doesn't work out, you must have enough money left to go back to school. Make sure that your idea will work before investing everything you have in it.

Work out exactly how much your business will cost to start. Draw up an estimate of costs like the one in Sample #1. If you are starting up a franchise, a good franchisor can probably provide you with a list of needed supplies and equipment and can give you some idea of where to get most of these items at a good price.

Then you need to expand your expense budget over the period of time you intend to do business. This cash flow forecast helps you understand how much cash you need and when you will begin receiving income. Ensure that there are always enough funds to meet your expenses and to allow you to continue in business for as long as you need. Worksheet #8 presents a cash flow set-up for a summer business.

c. FINDING START-UP FUNDS

You need to make sure you have adequate funds available at the right times for purchasing start-up equipment and for supplies. Unfortunately, start-up is probably the most difficult time for a business to find cash. Your business has a high demand for cash and no funds will be coming in from completed jobs. Therefore, managing your start-up requires careful planning and forecasting.

Students should look for start-up funds from these sources:

(a) *Personal savings:* Plan ahead and save up. Using personal savings allows you to avoid the possible restrictions of being in debt.

(b) *Government support programs:* Your business may qualify for a student loan for new business, often referred to as student venture loans.

(c) *Friends and relatives:* Parents or friends may be able to contribute toward your start-up costs. They are more likely to want to support you and stick by you if you get into difficulties and they can be much-needed financial allies.

47

(d) *Credit cards:* Interest charges are high, but if you only need a small amount of start-up funds, then credit cards can be a ready source of funds. You can pay back the amount owed over a period of time and conserve cash during your start-up period.

(e) *Bank loans:* Interest rates are relatively high and most students need someone to cosign the loan. If you take out a bank loan, you must meet the payments even if your business is not doing well. Failure to make your loan payments on time can affect your future credit rating and future loans or mortgages.

If all else fails, there are a number of loans and incentive programs to help young entrepreneurs get started. Your local government business service center can direct you to the right program or office for your area and type of business (see Appendix for addresses.) There is government assistance available to help small businesses get off the ground. You may be eligible for a low interest loans from your local bank or for a special arrangements loan with interest paid for a specified time only. Furthermore, most provinces and states offer youth-venture type loans that are interest free.

SAMPLE #1
ESTIMATING START-UP COSTS

Item	Price Range*		Actual Costs
Business registration:			
License	$ 0 to $ 60		$ 30
Permits	0	60	40
Registration	0	100	50
Basic office supplies:			
Basic stationery	0	50	35
Phone line set-up	35	70	50
Answering machine or service	30	100	80
Accounting and scheduling books	10	30	20
Basic office equipment:			
Computer	0	2,000	1,500
Fax machine	0	300	275
Insurance:			
Personal	0	200	150
Employee	0	200	150
Equipment and/or property	0	200	200
Damages	0	800	700
Equipment:			
Rented or leased	100	1,000	600
Purchased	500	2,000	1,100
Vehicle:			
Purchase and/or rental	0	3,000	1,000
Maintenance (per month)	80	300	100
Gas (per month)	30	100	50
Miscellaneous	40	80	60
TOTAL START-UP COSTS	$ 825 to $10,650		$ 6,190

* Price ranges are based on most common student service or product businesses. Actual values may vary depending on type of business and whether or not you already own items that can be used in the business.

WORKSHEET #8
CASH FLOW FORECAST

MONEY RECEIVED

	APRIL	MAY	JUNE	JULY	AUGUST	SEPT.	TOTAL
Forecasted sales	$	$	$	$	$	$	$
Loans							
Investor cash							
Interest from term deposits, etc.							
Other income — personal, etc.							
Total money received	$	$	$	$	$	$	$

MONEY PAID OUT

	APRIL	MAY	JUNE	JULY	AUGUST	SEPT.	TOTAL
Licenses and permits	$	$	$	$	$	$	$
Equipment							
Rental costs							
Office expenses							
Materials							
Employee payroll							
Promotions							
Debt repayment							
Insurance							
Miscellaneous							
Total money paid out	$	$	$	$	$	$	$

NET CASH (cash received minus cash paid out)

	APRIL	MAY	JUNE	JULY	AUGUST	SEPT.	TOTAL
Monthly income (+)/loss (−)	$	$	$	$	$	$	$
Total cumulative profit/or loss (includes previous months' total profit/loss)	$	$	$	$	$	$	$

8
FINDING YOUR MARKET

In order to sell your product or service, you need to find customers, or a market, interested in what your business has to offer. You need to understand who your market is and how your business can reach that market in the most efficient way. Learn all you can about your potential customers as well as your competition; get as much specific, detailed information as possible. Solid market research can save you a lot of time and money.

Your research can be broken down into two steps. First, identify and understand your customers: Determine the area, income, and demographic profile of your potential customers. Second, identify and understand your competition. Get to know their strengths and weaknesses.

The more precise you are about the type and level of competition and the kind of customer you are trying to attract, the more useful your research will be.

a. KNOW YOUR CUSTOMERS

You need to know what aspects of a product or service will attract customers to your business. In general, quality, service, convenience, and price are attractive features. Whatever your answer, your advertisements should focus on the advantages — not exclusively, but heavily. To find out what will appeal to your customers the most, you need to conduct extensive research.

1. Primary research

Primary research includes all the explanatory and specific information.

There are three basic means of conducting primary research: direct mail, telemarketing, and personal interviews. For most students, it is best to conduct personal interviews with people who have experience in your field. Get a variety of viewpoints before you spend any money on marketing. Whatever your methods, make sure your questions are short and to the point. There is no point in questioning someone you know will just say yes to support you. Look for people who can talk objectively about your idea and its advantages and disadvantages and give you constructive feedback.

You can contact local business people who have products or services similar to yours, or even friends and relatives, and ask for advice and information. Here are some examples of questions that you might ask:

(a) Do you think this is a marketable idea at the student-business level?

(b) Can you think of any consumer markets that would be good to market to other than the one I've outlined?

(c) Can you think of any significant competitors that potential customers may prefer to go to? Why?

(d) Could you suggest any way to make this business more marketable?

(e) What do you think is the best way to market to these potential customers?

(f) Do you think my goals are realistic?

(g) Would you use my products or services?

(h) Do you know of anyone else that would be a good person to ask about this idea?

2. Secondary research

Secondary research includes data assembled by government agencies, industry and trade associations, media sources, Chamber of Commerce, labor unions, etc. These are often in the form of reports, books, pamphlets, newsletters, newspapers, or magazines. This research is secondary because it is generated by companies or individuals outside your company. Secondary sources have three main categories: public, commercial, and educational.

Public sources are usually free and are most likely found in government offices and the public library. Commercial sources such as subscriptions to an association are usually costly and should probably be avoided by first-time student entrepreneurs. Education institutions have a great deal of information available through both personnel and libraries.

When you have completed the customer research properly, fill in Checklist #2 and #3 with the details of your market. The completed checklists will give you a short and concise description of your market for easy analysis.

b. KNOW YOUR COMPETITION

The second step in finding your market or niche is to understand what niches have already been filled. Therefore, researching the competition is your next step. Competitors can usually be found in the telephone book, trade directories, or by asking potential customers if they are aware of any other firms offering your product or service.

Try to analyze what makes a company's product or service different from the others and what makes a company profitable in your industry. Finding out what the average profit margin or sales value is helps you set realistic goals for your company.

Look at how your competition is advertising and who they are targeting. Is their advertisement hitting a good market or the only market? Are there customers who are left unsolicited?

Finally, think about what customers may like or dislike about your competitor's product or service. Are business hours inconvenient for many people? Is price an issue? Is selection of the company's product sufficient? Is there efficient customer service? Attention to these factors can help you develop a product or service that fits into your customers' needs more effectively.

While you research your specific competitors, you will also develop a thorough understanding of your industry. The following are the things that you must know about your competition and the industry as a whole:

(a) Which firms are you competing against? What are the names and locations of other firms you will be competing with?

(b) What alternative products and technology threaten the industry? For example, if you are a painter, how many people will decide to put up aluminum instead of painting their house?

(c) What are the current buying powers of customers? Is the economy low or high? Will people be looking for better prices or better quality? Will they have the money to pay for the service?

(d) What are the current economies of supplies? Do other companies have economies of scale (a decline in average costs per unit as the quantity of units bought or sold increases) and can you get competitive pricing from suppliers?

CHECKLIST #2
WHO ARE MY CUSTOMERS?

DEMOGRAPHICS

Age groups:
- ☐ 1 to 10
- ☐ 11 to 20
- ☐ 21 to 30
- ☐ 31 to 40
- ☐ 41 to 50
- ☐ 51 +

Sex:
- ☐ Male
- ☐ Female

Marital status:
- ☐ Married
- ☐ Single
- ☐ Common-law
- ☐ Divorced/separated

Yearly income:
- ☐ 0 to $20,999
- ☐ $21,000 to $44,999
- ☐ $45,000 to $59,999
- ☐ $60,000 to $84,999
- ☐ $85,000 to $99,999
- ☐ $100,000+

Education:
- ☐ Some high school
- ☐ High school
- ☐ College/university

Occupation:
- ☐ Professionals
- ☐ Technicians
- ☐ Educators
- ☐ Homemakers
- ☐ Retirees
- ☐ Managers
- ☐ Tradespeople
- ☐ Self-employed
- ☐ Students
- ☐ Unemployed
- ☐ Other _____
  _____

USER CHARACTERISTICS:

Purchase occasion:

_____

_____

Benefits sought:
- ☐ Quality
- ☐ Service
- ☐ Economy
- ☐ Convenience
- ☐ Prestige

Notes:

_____

_____

_____

CHECKLIST #3
WHERE ARE MY CUSTOMERS?

General geographic location:

_____

_____

Specific location:

__ City __ Town __ Suburbs __ Farms __ High-rises __ Other

Where would I be most likely to meet my customers on a regular basis?

_____

_____

How do customers shop for my product or service?

_____

_____

Notes:

_____

_____

_____

c. FINDING OUT MORE

Information for your market research can come from many places. Some excellent sources for students that cover business and customer information include the following:

(a) In the United States, the Census Bureau has information on demographics in its publications. Ask your local librarian for the relevant titles.

In Canada, Statistics Canada offers a wide variety of reports on virtually every industry. Many of these can be found at your local library.

(b) In the United States, the Small Business Administration (SBA) provides small businesses with informational publications at nominal fees. Check the telephone book for the office nearest you.

In Canada, The Federal Business Development Bank (FBDB) operates a program called Counseling Assistance for Small Enterprise. Consultants experienced in a wide range of businesses can offer expert advice and basic research.

(c) Trade magazines can give you a great perspective on competition, advertisement, and customer trends in your specific industry.

(d) Libraries can offer you a wide range of information. Librarians in public libraries are invaluable resources and can guide you toward government reports as well as association lists and current periodicals. Be sure to check your school business library since it will have information that can help you learn how to do market research effectively.

(e) Your local Chamber of Commerce or board of trade can often tell you a lot about your competitors, their products or services, and their locations.

In general, these information sources are a great way to find out more about your customers and competition. For more information, read *Look Before You Leap: Market Research Made Easy*, another title in the Self-Counsel Series. In addition, you may also want to contact some of the sources listed in chapter 17 on networking. Complete Checklist #4 to assess whether your marketing strategy has answered some key questions for your business start-up.

CHECKLIST #4
THINGS TO CONSIDER IN MARKETING SUCCESSFULLY

☐ 1. Who is going to buy your product or service?

_____

_____

☐ 2. Where will they go to get it or where do you have to go to get it to them?

_____

_____

☐ 3. When will they want to buy your product or service?

_____

_____

☐ 4. How much will they pay?

_____

_____

☐ 5. How much will they buy?

_____

_____

☐ 6. How will you sell or produce your product or service?

_____

_____

☐ 7. How much profit do you expect from potential market areas and when?

_____

_____

9

FINDING SUPPLIERS

In any type of business you need supplies, whether it is a one-time purchase of large equipment or materials that need constant replenishing. Finding the right suppliers is important to a business since your suppliers will indirectly affect the cost, quality, and reliability of the goods and services you are providing. As well, many more established and reputable suppliers are able to offer student entrepreneurs tricks of the trade and training that can help increase the efficiency and profit margin of your business.

a. HOW TO FIND A SUPPLIER

1. Good suppliers

Choose your suppliers carefully. Material costs affect your pricing of both products and services. The reliability and quality of your supplies ultimately affect your work.

Always remember that not all suppliers charge the same prices. Talk to several suppliers and get a good idea of what the average prices are for the materials you need. Some companies may charge higher prices than others. This does not necessarily mean that they are too expensive. You should consider paying higher prices if that supplier is able to offer you higher quality, faster and more reliable delivery, better terms for returning goods, and/or delayed or discount payment plans.

If the quality of your materials is an important selling feature of your product or service, then look for companies that have a brand awareness. Many suppliers offer advertising or packaging that proves

to the customer that you offer superior products or services.

In addition, since you are in the business of reselling the products and services you are buying, look for wholesalers to supply you and try to avoid retailers if possible. This saves you the wholesale/retail markup price. This can be difficult since many wholesalers may still be expensive because you are so small and do not have an economy of scale (i.e., you don't buy enough to get the discounted price). Sometimes, if you search out the right suppliers, you can get substantial discount prices even though you cannot order large quantities.

In general, look for the best value, not the best price. Try to deal with as few sources as possible and keep them as local as possible. This cuts down on record keeping and travel time and helps you stay organized. It is better to build a firm relationship with one company than to be just one of many numbered accounts to many companies. In the long run, you will probably benefit from discounts, extended credit, and a stable relationship with your supplier.

2. Finding your suppliers

It can often be difficult for students to find suppliers because of the short term of the business operation and the lack of economies of scale. However, several sources of potential student business suppliers include:

(a) *The Yellow Pages:* It lists the retail and wholesale suppliers of products or services, but it does not give any details as to the size of the companies, reliability, or quality of their supplies. For most students this is the first place to look. Contacting some of the suppliers listed in the Yellow Pages often leads you to more appropriate and useful suppliers even though the ones you contact may not directly be able to supply your business.

(b) *Potential customers:* Most customers have some idea of what they are looking for and may have seen it before somewhere else. Many times they are able to tell you where they saw the supplies and thus provide you with a possible supplier contact. Customer supplier referrals are helpful because they ensure that the customers you are hoping to attract will be pleased to see you using supplies from their referrals. This helps them feel more secure about the quality and reliability of your work.

(c) *Local public library:* Business and industry directories are available at your local public library and are a useful source. Generally, you will find the names of local manufacturers, wholesalers, and agents that deal in similar supplies.

(d) *Other companies in similar industries or competitors:* Since these companies will probably be using the same or similar suppliers, they already know whom to contact. Some companies are willing to help out a student entrepreneur and will offer you advice and put you in touch with suppliers. However, the drawback of competitor references is that some competitors may see you as a threat and be quite offended at your inquiries. However, most competitors are willing to help out a student.

b. USING YOUR STUDENT STATUS TO GET DISCOUNTS

It may sound strange, but the same lack of economies of scale that can hamper your wholesale discounts can often help you get discounts from retailers. You may be too small to deal with a large wholesaler, but large enough to get retail discounts. Even some smaller wholesalers will probably give you discounts if they know you are a student.

Try asking for discounts from local large retailers on supplies and equipment. Let them know that if they give you the discount you will promote their products to your customers and other business people. Also, let them know that they are helping out student enterprise and your profits help put you through school. Many retailers will give 10% to 40% discounts to student businesses if they know they will get goodwill from it. Most often, lines of credit are also available from these types of suppliers. Just ask!

A second and often overlooked way of getting discounts from suppliers is to take the time to find used or leftover supplies. There may be nothing wrong with these items; bigger companies overlook them because of their set procedures and processes for buying in specific quantities which are not consistent with what the supplier currently has sitting on the shelf. Most suppliers are glad to give you a deal on these supplies just to clear shelf space. Over the course of a summer or even a year, you may find that this can add up to thousands of dollars in savings — savings that you can keep as profit.

c. WORKING WITH YOUR SUPPLIERS

As a business owner, you will quickly find that it is important and profitable to keep your suppliers happy and to have a friendly relationship with them.

Since you are small and, as a student, will probably be in business for only a short time, seasonally or otherwise, it is best to develop a reliable friendship with one or two suppliers who will extend both discounts and credit to you, rather than dealing with many suppliers on a less personal basis. Use Checklist #5 to help you assess the benefits of different suppliers.

Finally, to keep your relationship with the suppliers professional and effective, always be honest and pay your supply bills on time. Let your suppliers know what's going on, and if you need advice or technical help, ask them. Especially since you are a student, most suppliers are willing to help you. After all, if your business does well, you will buy more supplies from them.

CHECKLIST #5
FINDING SUPPLIERS

☐ 1. Assess what supplies you need.

☐ 2. Search out suppliers through the Yellow Pages, by asking customers and competitors, or by using trade publications.

☐ 3. Assess the benefits of various suppliers:
__ Price
__ Distance from your business
__ Products or services offered
__ Sales terms
__ Current product or service goodwill that can help you sell
__ Reliability

☐ 4. Determine if there is any customer brand awareness for your supplies that could help your business sell.

☐ 5. Determine if you can get retail discounts that allow your supply costs to be comparable to wholesale, or if wholesalers will give you comparable prices to businesses with economies of scale.

☐ 6. Choose the most beneficial supplier based on all factors. Try to have as few suppliers as possible so that you can develop a strong relationship and sales discounts with the suppliers you do use.

10
ADVERTISING YOUR BUSINESS

Before you can design an effective advertising campaign for your business, you need to know who your customers are and what appeals to them. If you are still unsure, review chapter 8 for tips about how to conduct market research and learn more about your potential customers.

Your advertising should focus on the feature of your product or service that is most attractive to customers. Your product/service's price, quality, or convenience are all things that appeal to customers.

Now you have to reach your new market. There are many ways to reach your target market, from door-to-door sales calls to fliers, telemarketing, and even radio. But the best way to really focus your advertising budget is to get client feedback. Listen to what your customers have to say and fine tune your advertising message or techniques.

You should also consider the advertising strategies used by your competitors. Do they rely on printed materials and promotional fliers, local newspapers and magazines, radio, television, or a combination of these? Is their advertising working? Perhaps their reliance on one mode of advertising has failed to reach a segment of the market, or perhaps there is some other weakness in their advertising campaign. Since you will probably be spending a lot of time and money on advertising, you will find that thinking this through and preparing ahead can save you time and money.

a. CREATE A PROFESSIONAL IMAGE

While it is important for any business to present a professional image, it is particularly important for student businesses to do so. Many customers have extra concerns when considering doing business with a student. This is a direct result of the short-term nature and inexperience associated with many student-run businesses. Presenting yourself as a full-time "professional" business helps to allay these fears. There are many ways to present a professional image. Here are some ways to boost your company's professional image.

1. Business cards

Business cards are essential! They can be done at a fairly low cost and have many benefits. Being able to give a customer or supplier a business card quickly lends legitimacy to your business enterprise. As well, when customers are not going to do business with you right away, they will often keep a business card on file and call you later. The same is not true for most other advertising media.

A good business card should include your business name, address, telephone number, your name, and your position. There should also be something on your business card that quickly conveys what your business does and the qualities of your business. This can be anything from a logo to a slogan, but it should be memorable and catchy. Something that will remind a customer to look for your card even if they decide not to do business until several months later.

2. Portfolio and letters of reference

As you start to get some work behind you, try to get customers to fill out comment sheets or write short, concise letters of reference for you. As well, any work that you are particularly proud of should be photographed. Put your photographs and reference letters together in a binder. Your portfolio binder can become a great selling tool. Letting customers flip through a portfolio not only reassures them that you can do the job right, but it also lets them see exactly what you are capable of and establishes realistic expectations. If a customer sees that you have done similar work before and that previous customers have been pleased with your work, they will feel more secure and be much more likely to work with you.

3. Uniforms

You may think uniforms are beyond the budget of a small business. However, uniforms can be both simple and affordable. For example, have your staff wear the same color shirt. Buy everyone identical shirts and have them get their own pants or extra shirts. This encourages employees to take care of their uniform and keep it as clean as possible.

You and your employees should always present yourselves as clean, neat, and well-organized. Little details can make a big difference in how a customer perceives your business and influence their willingness to work with you. As well, it is important to note that when you are doing estimates or advertising, wearing a clean shirt and tie may seem extreme, but it tells a customer that you are serious about your business and care about what they think.

4. Customer service

All your customer interactions should be friendly and professional. When difficulties or disagreements come up, remember the old saying, "The customer is always right." Your job should be to please the customer. Pleasing every customer ensures that you get paid and may generate good business through word-of-mouth. Eventually, this creates sales without you spending any time or money on advertising. Remember this when things get tough; then it won't seem so difficult to say "We will be glad to do that for you" to customers who want things done their way.

However, when a customer is obviously wrong or misguided, don't just agree with them. Try to inform them in a courteous and polite manner.

Also, never put down your competition. In most cases this only serves to drive your customers away. If you know a competitor is lying or has a poor reputation, suggest that the customer contact the Better Business Bureau. Never tell customers that they should do business with you and not your competitors.

Finally, manners play an important part in successful customer relations. Always treat your customers with respect and be polite, no matter what problems come up or how much you may come to dislike them. As well, ensure that your employees do the same. Let your employees know ahead of time what is expected of them. Make sure that they understand that they must come to you immediately if they have any troubles.

b. USING YOUR STUDENT STATUS TO GET FREE PUBLICITY

Many newspapers, magazines, and local TV and radio stations are interested in student enterprises because such activities make great community and human interest stories. This is especially true if your business is very entrepreneurial or out of the ordinary for a student business.

Try and take advantage of this free publicity. Not only do newspaper articles help you advertise, but they also lend legitimacy and security to your practice and help customers feel more comfortable about doing business with your company.

The best way to generate free publicity is to make the media aware of your business. To do this, suggest that customers, suppliers, or friends contact the media for you. If you try to contact the media yourself, they will often ignore you because they know your purpose is either to get free publicity or to get an ego boost. It helps if you can coincide your media campaign with some major activity in your business. This helps the media see that there is a story beyond "just another average business."

Overall, this is a great idea that can generate increased business through word-of-mouth. If you proceed with care and tact, it can be a highly effective method for getting your business known.

c. HOW TO USE ADVERTISING MEDIA

The type of advertising media you use depends on your target market. However, since most student businesses start as short-term, small investments, cost is also an important factor. In general, try to find the advertising media that best reaches your market at the lowest cost in both time and money. There are a number of advertising media that lend themselves well to small-scale or low-budget businesses such as the part-time or seasonal student business.

1. Fliers

Fliers are the most common means of advertising a student business. They are inexpensive and they can be distributed to a large number of people very quickly. If you or any of your friends have access to a computer, there are simple programs that let you design fliers and other sales materials. Many universities and colleges have computer labs with laser printers.

Graphics-based software, such as CorelDraw, Adobe Illustrator, or Microsoft Word 6.0, lets you create logos, shaded boxes, and special typefaces. Have your original printed on a laser printer; this gives you a superior quality original which you can then take to a "quick-print" shop to have thousands of copies printed.

Basic desktop publishing books with sections on good design are available in libraries and bookstores. These books offer helpful design tips on working with text and images, choosing an appropriate typeface, and designing for maximum impact. You can save a lot of money by designing your own sales materials instead of hiring a designer or artist. If you find that you can't use computer graphics for special effects, you can still create eye-catching fliers using an attractive typeface and bigger text. You can also print fliers on colored paper.

The most important thing to remember when advertising with fliers is to target them well. A good flier distribution system is described in section **d.** below. In general, fliers should include your business name and phone number. The most prominent section of the flier should describe clearly what your company offers and why customers should call you. Always try to include a catchy logo or slogan that will help customers remember your business, even if they don't call for several weeks or months.

The biggest disadvantage of fliers is that most people get so many that they tend to ignore them. A typical response rate for a good flier distribution may be in the range of 2% to 5%. See Sample #2 at the end of this chapter for an example of a simple but effective flier.

2. Posters

Posters are a good idea if they are well located. They can be produced and distributed as simply and easily as fliers with minimal expense. High traffic areas that attract your target market are the most obvious locations. But plastering them up everywhere is only effective for some business types.

Student entrepreneurs should be aware of rules and regulations regarding the posting of advertisements. Many states and provinces have laws against posting advertisements on things like mail boxes, light poles, or buildings that are public property. Use common sense. Don't post advertisements that are obscene or have objectionable comments or graphics. Do not deface public or private property.

Get in touch with the local government agency or private organization that owns the area or property where you want to post your ad. This could mean your local public sector office like City Works, Parks and Recreation, or the local Chamber of Commerce. Rules will vary based on where you live. If you want to post your ads in a private store, simply ask the owner.

Remember, ignorance is not a defense and if you violate a local law you may find yourself having to pay a heavy fine. The poster shown in Sample #3 at the end of this chapter uses text as well as an illustration to get its message across.

3. Newspapers

Newspapers are great because of their quick, wide distribution. They do not, however, target your specific market and, depending on the size of the newspaper, advertising can be quite expensive. Don't take out newspaper advertisements unless you are quite sure you will get sufficient response to cover the costs of advertising.

Typically, classified ads in the "services available" section of a newspaper are the best place for student advertisements since they have high readership and are relatively low cost. Try to have your advertisement run toward the end of the week or on Saturday; typically, newspaper readership increases on the weekends and people will be thinking more about services or products they need, rather than trying to get to work and make money.

As well, if you make the newspaper aware that you are an entrepreneur and a student, you may be able to negotiate a discount with them. This is rare and applies only to smaller local newspapers, but it is worth a try if you feel that newspaper advertisements are the best way to attract customers to your business.

4. Magazines

Magazines are a good idea if your product or service is directed at a very specialized or commercial market. Most magazines are directed at very specific markets, and hobbies, special interests, or beliefs are things the magazine readers share.

Like newspapers, magazines are good because they have high readership and require little time to set up the advertisement. The only disadvantage of magazines is that they can also be quite expensive. Make sure you have well researched your potential return before investing the money it requires to advertise in a magazine.

5. The Yellow Pages

The Yellow Pages are typically the first place a customer will look for a product or service. However, it is only printed annually and you must commit to advertising with it for a year. This can be expensive. However, if you are planning on running your business all year or have a seasonal business that you intend to keep running for several years, this is also a great advertisement source.

To advertise in the Yellow Pages, you must have a telephone line and submit your ad four months before books are distributed. Depending on where you live, this date varies. Call its customer service department to find out the exact submission deadline for your area. Depending on the circulation, the monthly rate will also vary. For a typical 2" x 2¼" ad, the monthly price will vary from $24.00 (for a book with a circulation of 10,000) to $180 (for large metropolitan areas).

Make sure you know what you want to do and what you want your advertisement to say before you commit to a Yellow Pages contract. This advertisement will be representing your business for a long time and if it's not done well, it will end up being very costly and troublesome. The customer service department will also help you with the design of the ad and provide a detailed description of what they require. (See the sections on designing a flier and poster above.)

6. Telemarketing

Telemarketing is a great idea, but you have to be able to talk to people directly about your business. It is particularly well suited to service businesses, since many customers may not realize they can use your service until you point it out to them; let them know how helpful it would be to have your service. If you decide to telemarket, prepare a good sales pitch before starting your calls and be prepared to hear a lot of noes. Here is how your sales pitch may start:

> *You:* "Hello! It's (your name) from (your company) calling. How are you today?"
>
> *Customer:* "Very well, thank you."
>
> *You:* "We are a company specializing in (whatever it is that you do). We will be in your neighborhood this week and would like to offer you (a free estimate, a sample, information, etc.). Would there be a time we could (whatever you want the customer to agree to)?"
>
> *Customer:* "Yes," (or "I don't know," or "No").

> *You (if yes):* "Wonderful. Shall we say Thursday morning? I'll need your full name and address."

If the customer says that he or she doesn't know, ask if there are any questions or concerns you can answer. Ask when would be a good time to call back.

If they are not interested, ask if they know anyone who would be interested in your product or service and thank them for their time.

Whatever the outcome, your conversation should end something like this:

> *You:* "Thank you Mr./Ms. (customer's name). Good-bye!"
>
> *Customer:* "Good-bye."

Note: If no one is in when you call, try back later. Since you are likely to get many noes, this process can be fairly frustrating; keep at it.

If you are nervous about this kind of public speaking, there are clubs you can join to improve your speaking skills. Toastmasters is a popular speaking group and it has chapters everywhere. There are also continuing education courses for improving your speaking which are offered in the evenings. You will learn about voice projection and tonality, and build your confidence. Don't get discouraged as you start your telemarketing campaign as you will probably be successful at generating quite a bit of work this way.

7. Door-to-door sales calls

Door-to-door sales calls are also a very good idea for both products and services. However, the biggest disadvantage to door-to-door sales calls is that they take a great deal of time and energy. If there is another less time-consuming, and still cost-effective, way to reach your customers, you should explore it first. With door-to-door sales, be prepared to hear a lot of noes. Don't get discouraged.

You should have a good sales pitch prepared before you start going door to door. A short, clear, concise pitch that does not leave the customer with any yes or no questions is the best. Try to get the customer to give a full opinion rather than giving him or her the chance to merely say yes or no.

8. Free sample advertising

If you have a product that does not cost very much to produce, free samples are a great idea. This lets people know that you have a good product and that you can get it to them at a lower cost than your competitors. The major disadvantage of free sample advertising is that it *can* be costly and if your free samples do not go to well-targeted potential customers, it may not pay off.

9. Other types of advertising

Most other types of advertising are often too expensive or too long-term for student businesses. Radio, TV, and outdoor billboards are great, but unless you can get short-term, discounted contracts, don't even consider them.

d. DEVELOPING AN ADVERTISING ACTION PLAN

An action plan is a well-thought-out detailed plan of who your target market is, where it is, and how you intend to distribute advertising to reach that market. A good action plan includes the type of advertisement you are planning, an idea of its cost, and a rough date as to when you plan to distribute the advertisement.

Typically an advertising action plan has three stages. First you distribute fliers to areas you wish to telemarket or do door-to-door sales calls. Distribute the fliers one or two weeks before you call. This way potential customers can be thinking about your product or service before you contact them.

Flier delivery can be done by your mail carrier or by the more economical way — by you. This method of advertising keeps your product or service in customers' minds and starts them thinking about whether they could use your business.

Second, after the fliers have been delivered, do your active advertising, such as telemarketing or door-to-door sales calls. Contact the potential clients after they have had time to think about your business. Generally, they will be more responsive.

Third, make a list of people in certain locales who were particularly interested, as well as anyone who was interested but not immediately able to do business. Contact these people later since they are likely to do work with you.

Often a fourth stage can be included after you have done some work in the neighborhood or area where you advertised. As you finish the job, let people in the area know that you will be available. Prospective customers can see the quality of your work and make their final decision. Go door-to-door again and let them know that you are in the area and finishing up some work. Ask them if they would be interested in your product or service.

This variation on the door-to-door method, with slight variations to suit your individual needs, can work for almost any product or service, regardless of whether you are targeting businesses, households, or other organizations. Use Worksheet #9 to help you set up your own advertising plan.

WORKSHEET #9
PLANNING ADVERTISING

Type of advertising	Date	Target area/street name	Cost	Purpose	New	2nd	3rd
1.					☐	☐	☐
2.					☐	☐	☐
3.					☐	☐	☐
4.					☐	☐	☐
5.					☐	☐	☐
6.					☐	☐	☐
7.					☐	☐	☐
8.					☐	☐	☐
9.					☐	☐	☐
10.					☐	☐	☐

AQUA DYNAMICS

PRIVATE IN-HOME
SWIMMING LESSONS
WITH A QUALIFIED LIFEGUARD AND INSTRUCTOR

adults & children

all levels

FOR INFORMATION AND APPOINTMENTS
CALL: 555-5678
(Reasonable and negotiable rates)

11
ESTIMATING AND PRICING — HOW TO LAND JOBS

a. KNOW WHAT MOTIVATES YOUR CUSTOMERS

Customers always buy products or services for a reason. In general, most customers want to gain such benefits as convenience, better health, social acceptance, peer admiration, economy, value, and security from the use of a service or purchase of a product. Your product or service fulfills at least one of these buying needs, so estimate and price your service or product accordingly.

1. Product purchase incentives

For your product to be successful, it has to be useful, be of excellent quality, and it has to fulfill your customers' buying motivation. Purchase incentives for products include the following:

(a) *Unique benefits:* Analyze all aspects of your product; which features are unique and noteworthy? Attractive features can make your product stand out against the competitors'.

(b) *Fulfillment:* Make sure your product fulfills a specific need of the customers. Ensure that your product does what customers need or want and that it does it as well or better than the competitors'.

(c) *Dependability:* Make sure your customers feel confident about your product. It is important that a consumer feels that a product will last as long as expected, or at least as long as the competitors' products will last.

(d) *Ease of repair:* If your product is over-used or misused, can it be repaired or must it be replaced? Be sure that your product has a low maintenance cost and can be fixed easily and quickly.

(e) *Resistance to wear:* What sort of use can your customers expect the product to take: heavy duty, house duty, or light duty? It must be able to be used at least as much as customers expects to be able to use it.

(f) *Appearance:* Make sure that your product meets customers' tastes. Is the appearance of your product acceptable to the user?

(g) *Impression of quality:* Make sure your customers have a positive impression of your products or services. For most student businesses, this impression is based on the projection of your business and its products, and is a direct result of your ability to sell yourself and your business.

(h) *Quality standard:* Does your product meet the industry standards? You will want to make sure that your product either meets or exceeds the operating standards of your competitors' products.

2. Service purchase incentives

A successful service business fulfills a need, and if it is a quality service, makes customers feel good about having used it.

Incentives for choosing a service include the following:

(a) *Unique benefits:* What favorable aspects of your business, such as <u>location</u>, <u>hours</u>, or <u>cost</u>, supplement your service and make customers prefer your service over a competitor?

(b) *Fulfillment:* Make sure your service fulfills customers' needs; customers want your business to perform the service properly.

(c) *Dependability:* Be sure that your customers can be assured of continuous service and that your business can be trusted to perform its service well. Customers want to be sure that you will be there next week or a year from now and not just change your mind and not finish work or not finish it properly.

(d) *Appearance:* Will customers' tastes, such as professional-looking reports, be met effectively by your business? Be sure that you can present your service and the people who perform the service in a clean, neat, and professional manner.

(e) *Impression of quality:* Make sure that customers' impressions of the service are favorable; form a favorable reputation for your business as soon as possible. This is mainly accomplished by selling yourself well and presenting a professional appearance.

(f) *Quality standard:* Be sure that your business meets the established standards of your industry.

(g) *References:* Customers will want to see that you have positive referrals. Once you have started to produce work you should try to get letters of reference or photographs of your finished work to let your customers know that previous customers were happy with your service.

3. Additional purchase incentives

There are other purchase incentives that influence your customers. Take the following into consideration:

(a) *Knowledge of product or service:* It is important that your consumers know about the products or services your business offers. You must advertise your product or service to the right market aggressively and in a timely manner.

(b) *Availability:* Have proper and convenient hours of operation and have an accessible location.

(c) *Buying patterns:* Be sure that your customers do not have any buying patterns that will hamper their decision to buy from your business. If you are in an industry where this could be a problem (perhaps customers always choose certain brands or go to the same shops year after year), you should design your products or services to meet their traditional buying patterns as closely as possible.

(d) *Value:* Make sure that your customers feel that the product or service is affordable and competitively priced. Sometimes it may be necessary to discount your prices in order to meet a customer's perceived acceptable price range; other times it may be necessary to increase your price.

All of these purchase incentives should be addressed when you are contacting a customer, estimating your product or service, and attempting to advertise or sell your product or service to a customer. Different people will weigh these purchase incentives differently and it is important to feel out your customer and understand which incentives are most important to him or her.

b. SELLING YOURSELF

By selling yourself, you ensure that the customer will want to buy products or services from your business and not a competitor. Here are some basic tips to help you sell yourself:

(a) *Be confident in your decisions and statements:* This means enter into discussions enthusiastically and openly. The simplest way to do this is to not make statements or promises that you are not confident you can keep.

(b) *Be prepared for your presentations and questions:* This does not mean you have to know every answer, but be ready to present yourself professionally.

   If you don't know the answer to a question or are unsure, tell the customer you don't know but will find out. When you are presenting a possible contract make sure the contracts are well presented and clearly state what is being done, when it will be done, and how much it will cost.

(c) *Be genuinely interested in customers' questions and concerns:* It is often a good idea at the end of a presentation to ask the customers if there are any questions or concerns that you have not addressed. Let them know that you do not want to leave any questions or concerns unanswered.

(d) *Dress properly and be well-mannered:* Basically, this means that when you approach your customers, make sure you are clean and neatly dressed.

   Hold doors for them and take your shoes off when you go into their house. These small formalities say much about you and your business.

   For more tips about making a good impression, see *Business Etiquette,* another title in the Self-Counsel Series.

(e) *Follow up your sales calls a few days or a week later:* This lets the customer know that you really want their business and are interested to know if they have any concerns or questions.

(f) *Keep records of your customer interactions:* Remember customers' names or specific interests; it makes them feel that you care and that they are getting individual treatment.

   A customer may call you again two months after your first contact; being able to remember the person's name and his or her special concerns could make or break the sale. As well, by keeping good records you can go back and call customers who decided to wait for their purchase.

   A customer information sheet is included in Worksheet #10 to help you with this process.

WORDS TO SELL YOURSELF

Use the list of action words below when selling yourself and your product or service. Using action words helps you pinpoint what you can do, as well as helping you appear confident.

- advise
- analyze
- arrange
- assemble
- assist
- buy
- calculate
- care for
- categorize
- code
- collect
- communicate
- complete
- compute
- conduct
- construct
- contact
- contribute
- copy
- create
- deal with
- define
- demonstrate
- design
- develop
- devise
- edit

- encourage
- establish
- estimate
- expand
- facilitate
- generate
- handle
- identify
- illustrate
- implement
- increase
- initiate
- instruct
- interpret
- invent
- locate
- maintain
- manage
- measure
- modify
- motivate
- negotiate
- operate
- order
- organize
- outline
- perform

- plan
- prepare
- produce
- promote
- publicize
- recommend
- record
- regulate
- reorganize
- repair
- research
- revise
- select
- sell
- simplify
- succeed
- summarize
- supervise
- synthesize
- teach
- test
- train
- tutor
- unite
- upgrade
- verify
- write

WORKSHEET #10
CUSTOMER INFORMATION RECORD

First interaction date: _____

Last interaction date: _____

Customer name: _____

Address: _____

_____

Telephone: _____   Occupation: _____

Personal information

    1. Age group: _____

    2. Marital status: _____

    3. Children: _____

    4. Estimated income: _____

Purpose of interaction/customer's interest:

_____

_____

_____

Any work performed: _____ When: _____

Still interested in work: _____

When: _____

Important concerns:

_____

_____

_____

Comments:

_____

_____

_____

c. HOW TO PRICE YOUR PRODUCTS

The first step in setting a sales price for your product will be to work out what your actual costs to make and/or distribute that product are. Then you will want to add on a percentage of your start-up and operating expenses, such as telephone, business registration, etc. These two amounts give you your actual cost to produce that product. To determine your selling price, add an amount for profit.

Worksheet #11 has been included to help you with this process. It is best if you do the product price breakdown on a per-unit basis. This tells you where your main costs are in producing one unit of product, and by changing these basic costs, you can change your total cost for producing all your products.

d. HOW TO PRICE YOUR SERVICE

The first step in setting a selling price or rate for your service will be to work out what your actual costs are to provide that service. Then you will want to include an amount that can help you pay your operating expenses. These two amounts give you your actual cost to produce that service. To determine your selling price or hourly rate, add an amount for profit. Use Worksheet #12 to help you with this process. It is best if you do the service price breakdown on a per-unit basis. This tells you where your main costs are in producing one unit of service, and by changing these basic costs, you can change your total cost for producing all your service.

e. GENERAL SUGGESTIONS FOR ESTIMATING AND PRICING

Generally, as a student entrepreneur, you should look at competing products or services and price your product or service at or below the competition. This ensures that your business starts out competitive and does not suffer from lost business due to overpricing.

Sometimes you can consider pricing your product or service at a higher rate than your competition, but this should only be considered if you know you have a strong advantage or quality that people will pay more for.

In most cases the decision of how to price your product or service in relation to your competition should be based on sound research, such as customer surveys or industry market assessments that prove to you that you can be successful even at this higher price. Whatever price range you chose, the goal is to *meet your projected sales targets*. If your price is too high, you will not sell enough, and if your price is too low, you will not make enough profit; finding a balance can be difficult. Listed below are some general suggestions for optimally pricing your product:

(a) *Set up a system:* Set up your estimating and pricing procedures systematically so that you thoroughly understand the costs and profit potential before you enter into contracts. This way your customers understand that you have arrived at your price fairly and with justification.

(b) *Research:* Study the competition, consumers, and your market in general. Try to determine what, in your specific industry, makes a specific price work successfully.

(c) *Experiment:* Change your prices and rates and see what response you received from the customers.

(d) *Determine demand:* Determine your prices based on demand for your product or service. If you are booked up with customers for a couple of weeks, try raising your average rate 10% or so and see what happens.

(e) *Determine difficulty:* Determine your prices based on the difficulty of the job. The more difficulty involved or the more skills required, the higher the price.

(f) *Determine size:* Determine your prices based on the size of the job. Larger jobs will expect discounts since you are getting a lot of work from them in one shot.

(g) *Price competitively:* Price competitively but do not assume that your competitors have chosen the right price. If you can prove your product is better than a competitor's, sell it for more. If you want to generate sales volume, sell it for less than the competitor's.

(h) *Calculate profit margin:* Price so that you can make an acceptable profit and realize your goals.

(i) *Calculate credit payments:* If you are selling on credit, price slightly higher, about 2% to 4% higher, than if customers are paying you up front. This helps to alleviate the risk that you might not get paid, or that it will take a long time to receive payment. It also encourages up-front payment.

Materials:

Description	Quantity	Price	Total
_____	_____	$_____	$_____
_____	_____	$_____	$_____
_____	_____	$_____	$_____
_____	_____	$_____	$_____
_____	_____	$_____	$_____
_____	_____	$_____	$_____

Total material costs: $_____

Labor:

Activity	Total time required	Rate/ unit time	Total
_____	_____	$_____	$_____
_____	_____	$_____	$_____
_____	_____	$_____	$_____
_____	_____	$_____	$_____
_____	_____	$_____	$_____
_____	_____	$_____	$_____

Total labor costs: $_____

Total labor and material costs: $_____

Estimated operating costs: $_____

Expected profit: $_____

Selling price: $_____

(Selling price = Total labor and materials cost + Estimated operating costs + Expected profit)

WORKSHEET #12
COSTING OUT YOUR SERVICE

Materials:

Description	Quantity	Price	Total
_____	_____	$_____	$_____
_____	_____	$_____	$_____
_____	_____	$_____	$_____
_____	_____	$_____	$_____
_____	_____	$_____	$_____
_____	_____	$_____	$_____

Total material costs: $_____

Labor:

Activity	Total time required	Rate/ unit time	Total
_____	_____	$_____	$_____
_____	_____	$_____	$_____
_____	_____	$_____	$_____
_____	_____	$_____	$_____
_____	_____	$_____	$_____
_____	_____	$_____	$_____

Total labor costs: $_____

Total labor and material costs: $_____

Estimated operating costs: $_____

Expected profit: $_____

Selling price: $_____

(Selling price = Total labor and materials cost + Estimated operating costs + Expected profit)

12

DEALING WITH COMPETITION

When attempting to deal with a competitor, there are really only two options available — either you try to be completely different or you try to imitate them. Depending on your specific field, type of competition, and customer requirements, you will find that one way works better then another. Before you can do this, you must identify who your competitors are, what they are doing, and what type of competition you are in.

a. IDENTIFYING YOUR COMPETITORS

1. In general

A competitor is a company or person that hopes to attract customers in your consumer market to make a profit. You will quickly find that any company has a wide variety of competitors. You can easily identify many of your competitors by simply being aware of companies similar to yours in your community or by looking in the Yellow Pages or similar trade publications under the product type or service field you intend to offer.

However, remember that competitors can also include businesses that are outside your business field. For example, if you run a painting business, your major competitors will include professional and student painters. However, often overlooked are companies that install aluminum siding, eaves troughing, or vinyl windows.

Since you can tailor your product or service to out-compete other companies in your specific field, in many cases the "outside competitors" will be your major headache.

They change your market and have completely different traits that can be difficult to compete against.

As well, competitors can often disrupt a segment of your target market, such as households, businesses, government, or non-profit organizations. For example, many large firms have their own in-house window cleaners or computer consultants and won't want to use your services, no matter how cost-effective or professional you are.

2. In your business

Try using Worksheet #13 to identify your specific competitors. You can get competitors' names from many sources, but the best are the Yellow Pages, trade or industry magazines and publications, suppliers and potential customers. Make sure you are as complete as possible.

b. TYPES OF COMPETITION

There are two major types of competition facing student entrepreneurs: many small businesses (Competition A) and a few large businesses (Competition B). To deal effectively with these competing structures, you've got to understand their unique features. Most businesses face some degree of competition from each of these types.

Competition A is found in industries where many businesses have similiar products or services. The benefit of this type of competition is that any business can enter or leave the market with relative ease.

1. *What field of business is your company in?*

_____

2. *Who are your competitors in your field?*

(a) _____

(b) _____

(c) _____

(d) _____

(e) _____

3. *What related fields of business affect your industry or your company?*

(a) _____

(b) _____

(c) _____

(d) _____

(e) _____

4. *Who are your competitors in related fields?*

(a) _____

(b) _____

(c) _____

(d) _____

(e) _____

5. *What are the advantages and disadvantages of each of your competitors as your customers would see them?*

COMPETITOR	ADVANTAGE	DISADVANTAGE
(a) _____	_____	_____
(b) _____	_____	_____
(c) _____	_____	_____
(d) _____	_____	_____
(e) _____	_____	_____
(f) _____	_____	_____
(g) _____	_____	_____
(h) _____	_____	_____
(i) _____	_____	_____
(j) _____	_____	_____

This type of competition allows businesses to either specialize or imitate their competitors. House-painting businesses and window-cleaning businesses are examples of this type of competition. Companies offering similar products and services can often be differentiated by their different prices, quality, or range of services.

Competition B is found in industries where a few companies account for most of the industry's sales. Industries with this type of competition are typically difficult to enter and require careful planning. A student can only hope to enter the market by finding a very specific niche and filling it with a specialized product or service. Computer software businesses are an example of this type of competition. Competition B products and services can often be differentiated by their unique features, price, or reputation.

Depending on your specific field, you may wish to compete in different ways. The first step is to identify the types of competition you face. Then you need to determine the relative importance of each competitor and its effect on the market. List all your competitors in Worksheet #14. Then decide how serious a threat each one represents to your market and whether you can compete effectively.

Now that you know who your competitors are, the type of competition you are facing, and the variable importance of each, you can consider how to deal with them. As previously stated, your two choices are to try to be the same or to try and be different.

Your decision of which strategy to adopt really depends on your specific field and the strength of your competition. However, the following sections can help you understand how to use whichever strategy you choose — imitation or differentiation — to your advantage, depending on what you decide is best for your business.

c. HOW TO TAKE ADVANTAGE OF BEING DIFFERENT THAN YOUR COMPETITION

Being different than your competition is effective when your market is saturated or is becoming saturated, or when you can market your product or service as one that can outperform generally accepted products or services. Find your own niche. In addition, you must also create a different means to service that niche.

Typically, if you are different from your competition, and if your reliability and quality are equal to or better than the competition, you can charge more since you have an edge. As long as customers feel your business is professional and reliable, many people will pay more for this advantage.

Generally, planning out a business to be different than your competitors takes longer than planning one that is the same. You have to spend time finding new products, new services, or new ways to offer your products and services. As a result, many student entrepreneurs want to have some business experience behind them before they attempt to differentiate their business from the competition. When you are starting out, it is harder to recognize which differences can be capitalized on and how to capitalize on this difference.

d. HOW TO TAKE ADVANTAGE OF BEING THE SAME OR IMITATING YOUR COMPETITION

Being the same as your competition is usually beneficial in a market where there are accepted standards, such as set procedures for performing a service or specific features of a product. The similarity in products or services to larger, more accepted companies can help you establish the reputation of your business.

Being similar also means that you will likely have similar supplier and production

Competitor	*Type of competition*	*Importance:* How serious of a competitor is it?		
		Minor	**Moderate**	**Major**
1. _____	_____	❑	❑	❑
2. _____	_____	❑	❑	❑
3. _____	_____	❑	❑	❑
4. _____	_____	❑	❑	❑
5. _____	_____	❑	❑	❑
6. _____	_____	❑	❑	❑
7. _____	_____	❑	❑	❑
8. _____	_____	❑	❑	❑
9. _____	_____	❑	❑	❑
10. _____	_____	❑	❑	❑

costs, but since your student business will most likely have lower fixed costs than a full-time business, you should be able to price your product the same or below your competition. Thus, your business can be more economical, and if you produce your product or service with the same quality and reliability, this will ensure that you are very successful.

On the other hand, being similar to your competition does have substantial drawbacks in a saturated or nearly saturated market, since the competition from larger companies may overwhelm your abilities to convince customers that your company is worth doing business with. You have to compete with companies that are convincing customers full-time with larger advertising budgets than you.

Be aware and keep informed of changes and market opportunities. As always, you should try to find a niche or market segment and concentrate your limited time and funds on that market. If you reach this market early and keep in touch with it, you are much more likely to be successful and use your similarity to your advantage.

e. HOW TO AVOID BEING OUTSOLD AND STAY AHEAD OF THE COMPETITION

If you sit back and passively let the business go its own way, you may be outsold and assured of failure. Staying ahead of your competition means a variety of things. Not only must your company bring a better service or product to the customer, but you must also make that customer aware of your superior product or service in advance of your competitors. There are four main ways for a student entrepreneur to do this.

1. Be the first to start advertising

Being first is a major plus in business since customers will not have developed expectations or loyalty to a specific company. As well, if you are the first, most of the market will be unadvertised, which means you can quickly target the best market and contract the biggest deals before your competitors have even considered them. If you are in a seasonal business, this means that you should be the first to start advertising for that year or busy season.

2. Aim for a specific target market

Find out what your specific target market is and market it aggressively. Otherwise you will be stuck hoping some average consumer will buy your product and chances are you will miss out on the most profitable jobs.

3. Talk to your potential customers

Find out what products and services your potential customers are looking for and develop a solution (product or service) for those needs. Keep in touch constantly, every week or even daily, once your business has started production.

Don't let standing estimates or orders go unattended. Make the business interaction as friendly as possible so that customers want to deal with you and not other competitors.

4. Be aware

Get an idea of your market and the place you can fill in it. Keep aware of the limitations, laws, and restrictions on your type of business so that you never have to let a customer down because you couldn't do what you promised.

To summarize, the best way to stay on top of your competition is to find a fast, efficient, and cost-effective way to get your product or service out to your special niche. Do that better than your competitor by offering better service, price, and quality and you will assure yourself of fruitful sales and a profitable business.

13
DEALING WITH EMPLOYEES

To carry out all your company goals and strategies, you need help. Assess exactly how many employees your business is going to need and what functions they have to perform. Once you have done this and have worked out the other aspects of your business, you can start to determine what wages and benefits you can offer. It is only at this point that you should actually start looking for employees to fill those jobs.

a. QUALITIES TO LOOK FOR IN POTENTIAL EMPLOYEES

Who you choose to work for you is a critical factor in your business success. The people you need should have interests and skills consistent with yours. You must be able to get along with your employees and have them get along well with other customers and each other. To ensure potential employees have these necessary qualities, look for these skills, attributes, and abilities:

(a) *Flexibility:* You want employees who are prepared to be adaptable and will change their ways when necessary. This makes it much easier for them to fit into your team. Since you are on a tight budget, employees must be able to juggle many different jobs as required.

(b) *Openness:* You want as much communication as possible in your team. Try to find employees who aren't afraid to share their views and let you know what they are thinking and feeling. This makes it much easier to manage your employees and avoid frustrations and arguments.

Of course, this also means you have to be receptive and open yourself in order to encourage this behavior.

(c) *Ability to form and present ideas:* Since your employees really become the experts at the jobs they are doing, you want people who can analyze individual jobs and make good suggestions on how to do them better. As well, employees will be interacting with your customers and you want to be sure that they can present themselves intelligently and clearly to avoid misunderstandings.

(d) *Team work:* Ultimately, each employee will become part of a team. Thus, it is important that each one can work well as part of a team, offering his or her skills and abilities to improve the team as a whole, rather than working independently without any concern for the common goal.

(e) *Self-reliance:* While you want team workers, you also want people who are self-starters and who can work independently when required. If employees have to rely solely on each other all the time the team will be much less efficient.

(f) *Organization and time management skills:* Be sure that your employees are capable of organizing time well, and can analyze any problem that may come up in order to find solutions, rather than just waiting until someone else solves it for them.

(g) *Motivation/dedication:* These attributes show a concern for tasks. Ensure that potential employees are motivated and dedicated to their jobs, so that they will want to do the job well, with pride in the finished product, even when unsupervised.

(h) *Leadership:* You want to be the one in charge, but you will want to pick a senior employee who shows the most leadership ability to run things when you are not there. Other employees will not need such powerful leadership skills and in fact it may be better if you can find some employees who are more interested in being led, rather than leading.

(i) *Problem-based learning skills:* This skill represents employees' ability to learn by solving problems. You should look for employees who use problems as learning experiences and utilize feedback. This makes your team much more efficient.

(j) *Interpersonal skills:* Your employees need to have good interpersonal skills. Make sure your employees can communicate intelligently, clearly, and effectively, and that they are receptive to other people's concerns and opinions.

(k) *Reliability:* If employees do not come through with what they are expected to, when they are expected to, you are the one who must suffer the loss and explain to the customer what went wrong. To assess potential employees' reliability, look at previous job references and experiences to see if they have been reliable in the past. Ask them if there are any other commitments that might affect their job performance since this may reduce their flexibility and times they are available to work.

(l) *Comparable personality:* Finally, you want to ensure that prospective employees' personalities are consistent with yours. Ask yourself, "Will I get along and work well with these people? Will they get along and work well with the other team members or with customers?" Be sure your answer is yes before you hire, as personality clashes will decrease everyone's motivation and efficiency.

Use Worksheet #15 as a guide to the qualities you want to look for when you are interviewing. For more tips about interviewing and screening employees, see *A Small Business Guide to Employee Selection,* another title in the Self-Counsel Series.

b. BUILDING EFFECTIVE TEAMS: PEOPLE MANAGEMENT

First of all, student entrepreneurs should understand the value of job applications, job descriptions, and conducting interviews to select and hire new employees. Taking the time to ensure this process is covered effectively saves frustration and, in the long run, time. Worksheet #16 is an employee interview form that can be filled out by potential employees as the first stage of the interview process.

Second, it is important that student entrepreneurs recognize that there is a period of adjustment as new employees learn to handle their jobs. You have to train an employee, keeping in mind that in most cases a new employee will not do a job as well, or as quickly, as you (the owner) can.

You can increase employee productivity and enthusiasm in a number of ways. Being an enthusiastic manager who shows interest in what employees are doing is what works best for a small business. Employees are more relaxed and productive when the manager shows concern and interest in their happiness.

WORKSHEET #15
ASSESSING POTENTIAL EMPLOYEES

Name of job applicant: _____

Level of Skill, Attribute, or Ability

	1 (Low)	2	3 (Average)	4	5 (High)
Flexibility	1	2	3	4	5
Openness	1	2	3	4	5
Ability to present ideas	1	2	3	4	5
Team working ability	1	2	3	4	5
Self-reliance	1	2	3	4	5
Organizational ability	1	2	3	4	5
Motivation/dedication	1	2	3	4	5
Leadership ability	1	2	3	4	5
Problem-based learning skills	1	2	3	4	5
Self-interests consistent with the job	1	2	3	4	5
Interpersonal skills	1	2	3	4	5
Reliability	1	2	3	4	5
Personality	1	2	3	4	5
SCORE	___	___	___	___	___

___ **DON'T HIRE**   ___ **HIRE**

WORKSHEET #16
EMPLOYEE APPLICATION FORM

Specify position applied for:

1. _____   Salary expected: $ _____

2. _____   Date available: _____

Full-time _____   Part-time _____   On call _____   Summer _____

Why do you want to work for us?

_____

_____

_____

PERSONAL INFORMATION

Last name: _____   First name: _____   Initial: _____

Address: _____   City: _____

Province/State: _____   Postal/Zip code: _____

Telephone: _____

Are you legally entitled to work? _____

Social insurance/security number: _____

Describe any disability or medical condition that may interfere with your ability
to do the work for which you are applying:

_____

_____

EDUCATION AND TRAINING

	High school	College or university	Other education
School:	_____	_____	_____
Name and location:	_____	_____	_____
Dates attended:	_____	_____	_____
Graduated:	_____	_____	_____
Degree:	_____	_____	_____
Major field of study:	_____	_____	_____
Approx. grades:	_____	_____	_____

Knowledge of technical equipment: _____

_____

_____

Languages spoken: _____   _____   _____

EMPLOYMENT RECORD

Company name and address	Dates employed	Position/description of duties	Reason for leaving	Contact (supervisor's name and number)

REFERENCES

Name	Years known	Occupation	Complete address	Telephone

DECLARATION

By signing this application, I declare that the above information is correct and true and that this company has the right to investigate my statements. I agree that any false statement or misrepresentation in this statement will be grounds for dismissal from employment.

Date: _____   Signed: _____

A good manager is also a good listener. Often employees need help or have concerns that they might not always bring up in everyday conversation. Managers will often find that employees have great suggestions about how to do a job better, cheaper, or more efficiently.

When talking to employees and giving feedback, always try to first praise them for one or two things they are doing well before discussing areas where there is room for improvement. Help your employees understand what is required of them by setting standards. If the employees achieve your maximum standards, offer some kind of reward. Extra pay or time off can be incentives to strive for excellence.

Motivate your staff, but also do random spot checks. This ensures that things go smoothly even when you are not there. Getting people to work for you and getting them to work hard for you is easier if you hire the right people to begin with.

Industrial psychology offers two basic theories about why people perform well. One is that people work well if they understand what they are doing and why their job is important. Employees also work well if the job approach focuses on self-interests. Unless a job satisfies their interests and needs, neither fear nor persuasion can get employees to work well.

The best source for new employees is often friends and acquaintances. People recommended by your friends or employees are, in a sense, prescreened. Beware however, that hiring someone simply because he or she is a friend may cause you problems in the future and the ramifications could affect your personal life.

Whenever possible, structure the job so that the holder has a title; this makes employees feel that they are part of a team and gives their job some importance. Allowing employees to give feedback and input about how the company is run helps create a friendly, team spirit environment. Use bonuses based on production or achievement. End-of-summer lump sum bonuses work well because they encourage the employee to stay on the job all summer (helping you reduce training costs) and ensure that the employee maintains a high level of efficiency all summer.

In labor-intensive jobs, base pay raises on hours worked or production tasks accomplished to encourage employees to maintain consistency.

c. PAYROLL

Your employees want to be paid the proper amount, on a regular basis. This can be difficult if you are busy or keep insufficient records. Because of various government regulations and taxes, payroll in a student business can be a nightmare. Filling out and registering your business for payroll deductions is a long and technical task, one that is not well suited to the part-time or summer student entrepreneur. The repercussions for incorrectly deducting and remitting payroll taxes can be major and have a serious effect on employee cost.

Many banks now offer payroll services for very reasonable fees. These services take virtually all of the complication and technical problems away and are strongly recommended for the student business. To use these services, get in touch with a bank representative and provide the employee names, hours worked, and other government data and the bank will take care of the rest. They even issue checks and manage your employee wages for you. Usually, you will receive an overview statement showing what deductions were taken and how much each employee was paid. These data services are also very useful for your accounting needs.

On the other hand, if you have only one or two employees you may choose to do your own payroll to save the cost of a payroll service. You should be aware that businesses must register their employees with such organizations and programs as the Workers' Compensation Board, unemployment insurance, and old age pension plans.

Contact your local government and find out what the required registrations and deductions are for your area. Doing payroll yourself can have some advantages, such as keeping your expenses down, but if you have more than one or two employees, the bank's payroll service is usually the best choice, since in the long run it will save you a lot of time and frustration. Once you have used a payroll service you will quickly recognize that it is worth the money spent. It can improve your payroll accuracy and significantly simplify your record keeping. The risk of penalties for late payment of government remittances is completely eliminated and your employees' tax forms can be filled out accurately with the year end tax forms the payroll company sends to your employees. In the end, this service leaves you with time to concentrate on producing profit, not doing paperwork.

d. SETTING PAY LEVELS

In general, employees have to be paid a wage that will ensure they take interest and care in their work. However, if employee wages are set too high, the company cannot be competitive or profitable. In order to establish this balance, you must first understand what motivates people to work.

People work for both financial and personal rewards. Everyone needs a level of income sufficient to meet his or her needs. One way to establish your employees' needs is to ask them in an interview or on a job application form what rate of pay they expect and how many hours of work they want. This way you can ensure that their expectations are consistent with yours.

Employees will want to know that their pay is set in proportion to their skills and experience and the experience of the other employees. For this reason, it is wise to draw up job descriptions for each employee before interviewing him or her, and then decide on relative pay levels. This level should be based on the number of skills involved in doing the job, the experience of the employee, and the level of physical and intellectual labor required.

Personal rewards include a sense of achievement and feelings of safety and security in a job. These can be established by having good employee relations and by letting employees have a say about how things get done. If they feel they are important and needed, employees are much more likely to perform their jobs well than if they feel that they are unimportant and simply a means to getting things done.

Consider your cash flow; make sure you can meet your pay rates and produce a profit. Pay must be at or above the legal minimum wages set by your province or state.

Consider the supply and demand for workers. If there are many employees with similar skills out of work in the area, employees are much more likely to work for less. If jobs are abundant, then they may not perform well at low pay levels.

Consider your ability to meet your employees' desire for achievement and importance. Can employees feel that they are accomplishing something as part of a team? If so, you may be able to pay a slightly lower wage. If the job is not very interesting and requires continuous labor with no encouragement, you may need to pay them more. For a further discussion of what motivates employees and how to manage them well, see *Motivating Today's Work Force*, another title in the Self-Counsel Series.

14
ACCOUNTING AND RECORD KEEPING

Student businesses must keep records just like large or full-time businesses for both planning and tax reasons. However, it is usually sufficient for student businesses to keep legal and accounting records that are simpler and more concise than those of larger or full-time businesses. This chapter helps you understand the accounting and legal records required for running a student business.

However, I also recommend that you contact your local taxation office or organizations that deal with small business to be sure your records and methods are accurate for your province or state.

a. PURPOSE OF ACCOUNTING

The purpose of accounting is to measure, record, interpret, and report the financial condition and performance of your business. Accounting is required to prove all income and expenses claimed on your tax forms. To serve this purpose, business transactions are grouped into three categories: assets, liabilities, and owner's equity. Assets are the positive dollar value of a firm. Liabilities are the debts of the business and have negative dollar values. Owner's equities are the claims of insiders and are kept in the form of capital in the business. Good record keeping is important for more than just tax forms. If you maintain proper records, you gain the following benefits:

(a) You are better informed about the financial position of your business and are able to make better business decisions. Good records give you an accurate idea of what income and expenses you have at any given time. You are aware of which expenses require certain amounts of cash and how much cash is available for other investments. Good records prevent business decisions failing as a result of insufficient cash.

(b) You can acquire loans more easily. Most banks require at least a cash flow and balance sheet in order to give you a business loan. You have to have records for at least one year to support and create your financial statements form.

(c) You know how funds are being used and are able to use them more effectively. As your business grows, you can look back and see where your income is coming from. This allows you to better target the markets that are performing for you. Likewise, you can look back and see where your major expenses came from. This allows you to try and become more efficient and cost-effective.

(d) You have no trouble meeting legal requirements. Properly maintained records allow you to meet your government tax obligations.

b. LEGAL REQUIREMENTS

Legally, your accounting procedures must follow accepted accounting procedures. Generally, this means keeping track of both your income and your expenses.

1. Income records

Keep track of the gross income your business earns on a per-sale basis. Income records should show the date, the amount, and the source of income. You should also record how you received the income; for example, cash, cheque, services, equipment, etc. Sample #4 shows the invoice that I use for my business.

All income should be totaled every day. You should also keep a running yearly total. It is important to send receipts and/or invoices to your customers; this allows them to properly file their expense records and help you keep good records of income.

Key items to include on your invoices are:

(a) your business name, address, phone and fax number,

(b) your sales tax numbers (if applicable),

(c) the customer name and address,

(d) the invoice or purchase number,

(e) a short description of the product or service,

(f) the amount owing, including a breakdown of taxes, and

(g) the terms of payment.

2. Expense records

You should always get a receipt or invoice for everything you buy for your business. A proper receipt must show the date of the purchase, the name and address of the seller or supplier, the name and address of the purchaser, and a full description of the goods or services sold. Some cash register receipts may not show all this data and it is important that you quickly write any missing data on the back so that your records are complete.

Expense records are only valid if they are accompanied by a receipt. Like income records, it is important to keep a running total of per-job expenses, but it is usually only necessary to total such expenses at the end of every job, not every day.

Key items to have on your receipts are:

(a) your business name, address, phone and fax number,

(b) the supplier's sales tax numbers (if applicable),

(c) the supplier's name and address,

(d) the invoice or purchase number,

(e) a short description of the product or service,

(f) the amount owing, including a breakdown of taxes, and

(g) the terms of payment.

Accurate records allow you to quickly deduct your expenses from your income and give you an accurate profit figure.

3. Keeping your records

A general legal requirement for business records is that they be kept on hand for a specific length of time. It is a good idea to keep your records for a minimum of seven years from the end of the tax year to which they relate. Having records on hand not only helps you go back and analyze your business (if you run it for many years), but it also ensures that if the government decides to audit, you will have the necessary files. "I threw the records out" is not a valid excuse, since in most countries business owners are required by law to keep records for a specific amount of time. Call your local taxation office if you want to know exactly how long you have to keep records in your district.

c. BASIC ACCOUNTING JOURNALS AND HOW TO USE THEM

The following items are suggested as the core accounting records you should be keeping for your student business. Basic accounting journals and receipt books can be purchased in most stationery and office supply stores. There are also a number of simple computer programs, such as Quicken, which make small business accounting quick and easy for student entrepreneurs. These programs also prepare invoices and financial statements quickly and easily and are a great idea if you have a computer.

1. Budget or financial plan

Setting up a potential financial plan is the first thing you should do after deciding on your new business idea. Your plan should be a month-by-month estimate of your sales and expenses. This helps you determine your expected income and make decisions about borrowing money. Once you start your business you can compare the actual figures with your estimated figures. This gives you a good idea of your potential to meet your goals early enough to make changes if things are not going right.

2. Payroll

Maintaining payroll records is discussed in detail in chapter 13. If you decide to have an outside company take care of your payroll, you will have to follow their suggestions.

3. Beginning and year-end reports

At the beginning of each business and the end of each summer or year that your company operates, you should complete a balance sheet and an income statement. This helps you calculate the performance of your business and report your income accurately for government records. An income statement is shown in Sample #5 at the end of this chapter. You can adjust the format of your income statement to reflect the nature of your business. See Sample #6 for a balance sheet.

4. Daily journal

It is a good idea to keep all your original receipts in an envelope, listed by month in case you need to produce them in the future. In addition, you should also keep a simple record of detailed receipts and payment, often called a journal. You can record these as you receive them and you will be able to

see exactly how much was paid out and how much came in every day. You should use a columnar accountant's pad and start a new one every month or day depending on how many transactions you have. A daily journal is shown in Sample #7.

5. Job report

This is a report that simply keeps track of all your expenses for a given job. You can quickly calculate the exact profit on the job and compare it to the estimated profit on your estimate form. If you find you are having trouble meeting your estimates, this form will help you identify the reasons for the extra costs. Keeping such a form will help you be more competitive and identify if things begin to get inefficient. After all, a successful business is built by having successful jobs, one after another. A sample job report is shown in Sample #8.

d. SOME BASIC ACCOUNTING EQUATIONS

There are several basic accounting equations to keep in mind when running your business. These equations can help you understand your financial position. Being able to accurately discuss your business's financial situation puts you in a much more knowledgeable position when you talk to your banker, franchisor, or others who may be interested in how your business is performing.

1. Assets equals liabilities plus owner's equity

Assets = liabilities + owner's equity: This equation is used on a balance sheet. Owner's equity is the value an owner has in his or her business. Liabilities are any debts the business owes to other companies or people. Since liabilities are negative in value, they decrease the owner's equity. The resulting assets are the final value of the owner's value or equity in the business after all debts have been paid.

2. Net profit equals revenues minus expenses

Net profit = revenues - expenses: This equation tells you how much money you have made after paying all your fixed and variable expenses. Your net profit is the total amount of money you get to keep, before taxes, for a fixed term of business operation.

3. Gross profit equals net sales minus cost of goods sold

Gross profit = net sales - cost of goods sold: This equation helps you calculate your profit before taking into account your fixed expenses. You can apply this equation to individual jobs or contracts to see if your actual gross profit is equal to, less than, or greater than your estimated value. This helps you evaluate your efficiency and break down where your money is going.

e. SALES CONTRACTS

One way to ensure that customers pay for your product or service is to have him or her sign a contract. The contract sets out what you will do for the customer, the total cost, the time for delivery or completion, applicable sales taxes, the date that payment is due, the method of payment, and any other details that need to be confirmed in writing.

If your business is going to provide a service over a long period, such as over the summer, or there will be a gap between the time the customer orders your product and the time that you can fill it, having a sales contract or service agreement drawn up beforehand is a good idea. Sample #9 shows an example of a basic contract for a student business. To be sure that any agreement you enter into is legally binding, have a lawyer check out your agreement. Making sure that your business is protected is always worth the cost.

DS ENTERPRISES

111 A Avenue
Buytown, Anywhere, L0G 0H0
Ph: 905-555-3079
Fax: 905-555-9013

INVOICE NO:
DATE:

To:

SALES PERSON	DATE STARTED	DATE COMPLETED	TERMS

QUANTITY	DESCRIPTION	UNIT PRICE	AMOUNT

	SUBTOTAL	
	SALES TAX	
	TOTAL DUE	$

Please make all checks payable to: DS Enterprises
If you have any questions concerning this invoice, call Dave Schincariol, 905-555-3079

THANK YOU FOR YOUR BUSINESS!

SAMPLE #5
INCOME STATEMENT

	WEEK 1	WEEK 2	WEEK 3	WEEK 4	WEEK 5	WEEK 6	WEEK 7	YEAR TOTAL
SALES								
Service A								
Product A								
Service B								
Product B								
TOTAL INCOME								
COST OF GOODS SOLD								
Labor								
Materials								
Miscellaneous								
TOTAL COST OF GOODS SOLD								
GROSS PROFIT								
EXPENSES								
Advertising								
Telephone								
Administration								
Office								
Payroll - Unemployment Ins.; etc.								
TOTAL EXPENSES								
NET PROFIT BEFORE TAX								
Tax								
NET PROFIT								

BALANCE SHEET

ASSETS		Amount	Total
Current Assets			
	Cash		
	Bank Accounts		
	Accounts Receivable		
	Inventory		
	Prepaid Expenses		
	Other		
	TOTAL		
Fixed Assets			
	Equipment		
	Machinery		
	Vehicles		
	Computer		
	Other		
	TOTAL		
TOTAL ASSETS			
LIABILITIES			
Current Liabilities			
	Loans		
	Accounts Payable		
	Other		
	TOTAL		
Long Term Liabilities			
	Long Term Loans		
	Leases		
	Other		
	TOTAL		
TOTAL LIABILITIES			
OWNER EQUITY			
	Capital		
	At start		
	Investment		
	Profit (loss)		
	TOTAL (minus withdrawals)		
	Withdrawals		
	TOTAL NET WORTH		

SAMPLE #7
DAILY JOURNAL

DATE	CUSTOMER/PAYEE	CHECK #	INVOICE	AMOUNT	TAX	TOTAL	DESCRIPTION

SAMPLE #8
JOB REPORT

JOB NAME:				
CATEGORY	**AMOUNT**			**TOTAL**
INCOME				
Gross Sales				
Income - Other				
total income				
EXPENSES				
Advertising				
Vehicle - fuel, etc.				
Equipment				
Office				
Rental				
Materials				
Employee Wages				
Employee Deductions				
total expenses				
GROSS PROFIT (LOSS)				

June 18, 199-

I, Joe Customer, of 188 Hamilton Street, Buytown, Anywhere L0G 0H0 [ph: 905-555-6789], hereby agree to purchase the following product/service at the stipulated price from ABC Student Business located at 123 Profit Road, Buytown, Anywhere L0G 0H0 [ph: 905-555-7622].

Job description:

1. _____ Price: $_____

2. _____ Price: _____

3. _____ Price: _____

4. _____ Price: _____

These products/services total $_____ including taxes. Payment is due immediately upon completion of the above jobs. The contract constitutes the entire agreement of the parties and no other understanding shall be valid unless in writing. All payment will be made payable to_____.

I hereby agree to the contract and acknowledge receipt of a copy of this contract.

_____   _____

(Sales agent for ABC)   (Purchaser)

Accepted by ABC Student Business by _____

* Note: All contracts should be reviewed by a lawyer.

15
TAXES

As a business person, you have to be aware of tax laws as they apply to your business. Unlike a conventional job, it is ultimately your responsibility to make yourself aware of these laws and pay the necessary taxes when due.

Every student business is unique and will have different expenses to deal with. In the United States, contact the local office of the Internal Revenue Service (IRS). They can provide many helpful pamphlets on various aspects of taxation.

In Canada, contact your local Revenue Canada office. You'll find the listing in the Government of Canada section of your local telephone directory.

Also check your school library or public library. There are many books on tax and small business that may save you time and money. Check the copyright dates of the books to ensure the information is up-to-date.

Remember, if you are audited you are legally expected to have accurate, clear, and complete records and to have met all legal requirements. Claiming ignorance of the law will not help you in the least. For information about what is required, contact your local tax office or government small business service center. (See the Appendix for addresses.) For more specific information, discuss your concerns with an accountant or seek legal advice.

a. TAXES IN GENERAL

For business purposes, taxes fall into three categories: income, sales, and property.

1. Tax on income earned

If your business is a sole proprietorship, you will include the income (or loss) of the business in your personal income tax return. Likewise, in a partnership, the owners include their share of the income (or loss) of the business in their personal income tax return, similar to any other income source. Alternatively, if the business is a corporation, it is subject to special federal and state/provincial corporate income tax. Information about corporate income tax should be obtained from an accountant.

Sole proprietorships and partnerships are generally taxed at around 20% to 50%, depending on the income level of the owner. Corporations are usually taxed at around 46%; since they exist as separate legal entities from the owners, the owners' income does not affect the corporation's tax rate. Since most students have limited income outside the business, and the business is generally only part-time or seasonal, students can expect their income taxes to be in the lower range.

2. Sales tax

There are many different kinds of taxes on sales and it is best to contact your local tax office to find out which ones apply to your business. However, in general, the federal government levies general sales tax, excise tax, and customs duties. Individual provinces or states also have their own sales tax. It is your responsibility to collect this tax from every job that is taxable and to pay this tax at regular and specified intervals.

You can find out if your business is subject to any of these taxes by contacting one of the business offices listed in the Appendix, or by looking up the name of the tax in the government section of your local telephone directory.

3. Tax on ownership of property or buildings

This is only a concern if you own a building or property and probably doesn't apply to most students. The tax is usually levied by the municipal government and is based on the size and value of your property and building.

b. STUDENT BUSINESSES AND TAX

The amount of tax you will have to remit depends on your type of business and sales level. You can legally try to minimize your taxes through good planning, consultation with professionals, and by learning about any laws and procedures. The primary means of decreasing your tax level is by taking your maximum deductions. This can only be done through careful and complete record keeping.

A self-employed student is allowed tax deductions similar to those a student would receive if he or she were employed by someone else. But, unlike a conventional job, there are additional tax deductions for student entrepreneurs. These additional deductions primarily include deductions for expenses incurred in connection with generating income and servicing your business equipment and vehicles. However, student entrepreneurs can only claim these deductions if they can provide receipts. This section discusses deductions that can be made from your net or final profit. To calculate this amount, see chapter 14 on accounting. Some of these after-net-profit deductions include deductions for transportation, depreciation, advertising, home office, entertainment, research, and training.

1. Transportation

You can deduct your actual expenses associated with setting up and managing your business, as well as those costs for delivery and shipping. For most entrepreneurs this would include such things as gas, oil, maintenance, depreciation, and insurance. But you can do this only as long as those expenses are related to expenses for use in the business. To help you keep proper transportation expense records, create a car expense book and record specific expenses on a daily basis, including the amount paid out, mileage traveled, and what the expenses were for.

2. Equipment depreciation

Equipment is a substantial cost of doing business and student entrepreneurs should be aware that most provinces and states have rules about claiming equipment deductions. The business owner may depreciate the cost of the equipment over a period of several years. The depreciation schedule is usually similar to the following:

Year 1: 32%
Year 2: 20%
Year 3: 19%
Year 4: 15%
Year 5: 14%

Depending on how long you intend to run your business and how much equipment you purchase, this may or may not be a significant deduction.

Also, depending on how the equipment is paid for (renting, leasing, outright purchase), the amount that can be deducted will vary. In most provinces and states, a rental or leasing expense for equipment is 100% deductible in the year it is incurred. Conversely, an outright purchase of equipment can usually be deducted in the form of depreciation over several years. Depreciation and deduction rules may change depending on where you are doing business, but the important point is that most equipment expenses can be deducted from your taxes at some point. To get an outline of the rules regarding equipment deductions, contact your local government small business office listed in the Appendix.

3. Advertising expenses

Advertising expenses typically include such things as fees for printing fliers and payroll for telemarketers. Basically, any expenses that are directly associated with informing your potential market about your business products and services are deductible as advertising expenses and are generally deductible up to 100%. The important thing to remember in claiming advertising expenses is that the advertisements you are claiming deductions for must be paid and used up in the fiscal period for which you are claiming deductions. If the advertising expenses are for future use, they must be used as future deductions.

4. Home offices

Offices in the home are generally subject to certain tax restrictions. But you probably qualify for deductions if you use a portion of your home as the principal place of business. Deductible amount calculations are based upon the percentage of your home used for business purposes. Items that can usually be deducted include repairs, cleaning, mortgage, interest, and property taxes. If you pay rent, you can also usually deduct a percentage for rent. To get a list of the appropriate deductions in your area, contact your local government small business office listed in the Appendix.

5. Entertainment

Any expenses associated with promoting the business and motivating employees or other interested parties are generally deductible, but usually only up to around 80%. These types of deductions must be reasonable and, if excessive, often provide a point of contention with tax auditors. A good rule of thumb for student entrepreneurs is to not let this type of deduction exceed more than 6% or 7% of your total deductions. However, depending on what kind of business you operate, they could be much higher. Accountants are generally the best people to advise you on whether your entertainment expenses are reasonable or not.

6. Other deductibles

Some applicable deductions that are often overlooked by student entrepreneurs include necessary preliminary expenses to set up business such as permits and registration, research costs, and employee hiring and training.

Depending on your type of business, there may be other deductions available to you. In most cases, deductions are just a matter of common sense. Ask yourself if this was a necessary expense to run your business or to generate profit. If the answer is yes, some percentage of it is probably deductible.

Just remember, you must keep all receipts for your deductions and they are only deductions if they are reasonable and incurred for the purposes of producing income.

c. HOW DO I REPORT MY BUSINESS INCOME?

As described above, you should report income as business income if, and only if, it is income from any activity you carry on for profit or with a reasonable expectation of profit. The two most important things to remember about reporting business income are that:

(a) in most cases, business income must be reported in the same fiscal period you earn it; it does not matter when you *receive* the income, and

(b) you deduct expenses in the fiscal period you incur them, whether you *paid* for them in that period or not.

Most often a cash flow report can help you report your income and expenses accurately (see chapter 14). For the specific means and ways of reporting the business income section of your tax return, refer to the income tax guide for that year. Most personal tax return forms refer to this section as income and expenses from a business.

Most corporations and some partnerships require special business income tax forms. Always consult an accountant if you are filing an income tax return for a corporation or a partnership.

16
JUGGLING SCHOOL AND YOUR BUSINESS — TIME MANAGEMENT

a. SKILLS TO HELP MANAGE SCHOOL AND BUSINESS

Managing life as a student and life as a businessperson can be challenging, especially when you try to fit in a social life. You may have your own system for managing your time in school and your social life. However, with the added responsibilities of running a business, it becomes even more important that you effectively manage all three aspects of your life — school, business, and social life — in order to be happy. Here are a few ideas that many student entrepreneurs find useful in managing their time:

(a) *Prioritize your commitment and responsibilities:* Do schoolwork when school is important and business when business is important. Don't let your enthusiasm for your new business overtake the long-term importance of doing well at school.

(b) *Keep a time planner:* A daily, weekly, or monthly list of what you have to do, and when, helps you manage school and business. This helps you avoid being overwhelmed by having to do two things at the same time or not leaving enough time to do things properly.

(c) *Be realistic:* When planning out your time, be realistic about how long things will take you. It's always better to give yourself a little extra time to allow for unforeseen problems. If you plan to allow a little extra time for each task or activity and it doesn't take as long as you planned, you have free time to get ahead on future things or to just relax and take a break.

(d) *Develop an organized filing system:* You will quickly accumulate a great number of documents, forms, and records that you will have to be able to find easily and frequently. A portable filing case or cabinet is a great idea for students because it lets you take your files with you no matter where you are. Having a proper system for organizing your documents saves you time and keeps important information at your fingertips.

(e) *Develop an organized message system:* Since you will be communicating with a fair number of people in your business, you need some way to retrieve messages quickly and efficiently. This ensures that you are not delayed by other people or doing the wrong work at the wrong time.

(f) *Avoid distractions and disturbances:* Stick to your daily plan and don't let telephone calls, the TV, or the like distract you until you have completed what you planned to do that day. Study or work on your business in a place where you know you won't be bothered; going to the library and doing your work there is often a good idea.

(g) *Group tasks:* Divide tasks by area, time, or activity. This helps you do things more efficiently. Lumping things together takes you less time than if you had to do them all individually.

(h) *Know your limit:* Know when you have too much to do and do not take on any more work until you can handle it. This helps you avoid frustration and ensures that the work you do, be it school or business, is done properly.

b. KNOW WHEN TO GET HELP

If you're going to manage your time well, you need to take a proactive stance. Plan ahead, get help when you need it, and delegate tasks to others; these are crucial steps to making sure you balance all the activities in your life. This is a challenge you face not only at the start-up stage of your business, but in day-to-day operations and possibly also at some future date if you decide to expand your business to a full-time enterprise.

1. Be proactive

Being proactive simply means that you think ahead and plan things out in advance. If you are following the suggestions in this book properly, you have already acquired the proactive habit. This can save you immeasurable frustration and prevent you from ever having to rush or not being able to complete something properly. Being proactive is perhaps the foremost trait that can help student entrepreneurs manage school, a business, and a social life all at once.

2. Get help

No one can meet every goal or be successful at solving every problem alone. When you are having difficulties, don't be afraid to elicit help from those who have more experience or education than you. This goes for business and school. Often others can help you solve problems better and faster than if you try to tough it out on your own.

3. Delegate effectively

The ability to delegate effectively is often a learned trait. However, you should recognize it as a definite advantage in time management. Not only can you delegate tasks to employees or others with an interest in your business, but often friends or family are willing to help you out of a tough spot.

Take the time to assess other people's abilities and determine whether they could assist you or take on one of your business tasks. In terms of your business, it will mean time saved for you and, in turn, a better end product or service.

c. WHEN DO I START PLANNING MY BUSINESS?

It's never too early to start planning your business activities. After you know what kind of business you want to run, where, and how, pick a date that you want to start actually doing business. You should start planning your business set-up, finding suppliers, and finding customers at least six to eight weeks before that date. This ensures that you have enough time to thoroughly think through the start-up process and follow the steps presented in this book.

In most cases you will find that this means you have to start planning your business during school. Dedicating time only to school and time only to business is the best way to concentrate on both and do both properly. Spend time organizing your business on weekends, holidays, or at times when your academic workload is low. Never rush your set-up or allow your enthusiasm for your new business to compromise school.

17
NETWORKING

a. THE BENEFITS OF NETWORKING

Business contacts can be invaluable sources of new ideas and opportunities. Many business contacts can offer advice based on their skills, education, and experiences which can help you decide what business to run, as well as help you set up your business and manage it.

A student entrepreneur has the distinct advantage of having the many high school, university, or college resources and staff to use and contact in developing business ideas and managing problems.

In addition, everyone has a variety of personal and social contacts that they find useful. Consider your relatives, friends, or friends' parents as possible sources. Chances are most people either know useful people or have acquaintances that do. Take advantage of these contacts.

Listed below are a number of contacts student entrepreneurs will probably find useful:

1. Other entrepreneurs and mentors

Whether they are in big business, small business, in your industry, or in another field, these people can often answer questions for you and give help based on their experience. Generally, if you get to know them well, they may help you on an ongoing basis. As they get to know your business better, they will be able to provide very specific answers to your questions. If these people are in a similar type of business they can often serve as guides or mentors.

2. Business professionals

Depending on what services you need and the type of business you are in, you will find it useful to consult the following professionals or experienced business people:

(a) *Lawyers*: A lawyer can help you with any of the legal considerations involved in starting your own business. However, unless you have a friend who is a lawyer, typical lawyers' fees range from $50 to $150 an hour and can be costly for a student entrepreneur. Most universities offer a free legal aid and information service to students and they may or may not be able to help you with your business problems. Remember, always get a lawyer to review any agreements or contracts that concern your business.

(b) *Accountants:* An accountant or bookkeeper can help you keep good ongoing records as well as offer advice on preparing your income tax. Unless you have a friend who is an accountant and who will give you a special rate, accountants' fees typically range from $25 to $100 an hour. It may be worthwhile to pay for a qualified accountant if your business is going to continue for a prolonged period of time or if you have substantial sales to account for.

(c) *Insurance agents:* Proper insurance is critical to the risk management of a new student business. A good broker can help you assess your insurance needs and recommend the appropriate coverage for you. Agents and brokers generally will not charge for their services since they make their money from the insurance investment.

The best way to maximize your use of these professionals and keep your expenses down is to have a good idea of what you want from them before you make contact. Get to know your obligations and responsibilities and be clear about your problems and needs, so that these professionals can help you quickly and easily.

3. Background people

(a) *Professors and teachers:* These people can offer you a wealth of knowledge from both theoretical and practical experience. Since you are a student, they often will be happy to talk to you and you will get quite a bit of advice at no charge. If you bring them specific problems, many times they will have the knowledge to recommend an appropriate course of action or can refer you to other professionals.

(b) *Human resource managers:* Chances are you know someone who is either directly involved in human resource management or has had experience with it. It doesn't matter whether they are from government, health care, big business, or small business. You can make use of their knowledge and experience in hiring, managing, and dealing with employee problems that may come up. Usually they have faced similar problems and if they know your business well, they can give you very accurate and useful information on how to handle personnel problems.

(c) *Scientists:* If your business is in the technological or scientific field, scientists are the people you should consult for specific technical advice. They may be able to help you establish contacts with the appropriate suppliers and customers. Since you are a student, they may be much more willing to talk to you free of charge.

(d) *Engineers:* If your business requires technical knowledge about construction, mechanics, or chemistry you may find contacting an engineer useful. They can provide you with technical knowledge and explain the feasibility of your ideas, possible problems, and pitfalls. Sometimes they can help you make more specific contacts that can help you develop a product or find suppliers and customers.

(e) *Tradespeople:* Plumbers, carpenters, welders, electricians, and other tradespeople can also help you. Depending on the type of business you are in, you may find their services useful. Unless you can get a special rate from a friend in the trade, tradespeople will probably charge between $25 to $50 an hour. Depending on where your business is located, local laws may require that you hire certified tradespeople to do certain jobs, or have your work officially inspected.

(f) *Seniors:* There is nothing better than the opinion of someone who has been around long enough to see it all. Older people can often offer general advice on business ideas and strategies based on their long history of personal experiences and simply being around to see things happen.

See the Appendix for addresses for start-up help and specific questions. See section **b.** for the names and addresses of organizations that specialize in helping student entrepreneurs develop their entrepreneurial skills, start businesses, and manage them effectively.

b. ORGANIZATIONS AND PEOPLE THAT CAN HELP STUDENT ENTREPRENEURS

1. Junior Achievement (Grades 5 to 12)

Junior Achievement (JA) is an international non-profit organization with local chartered organizations from coast to coast. Their main support is from companies, foundations, service clubs, and individuals. JA offers programs taught by experienced volunteers from the business community. Their primary goal is to help kids develop skills that can be applied to their careers and help make their transition into the business world successful.

As a student participating in JA, you'll learn business basics as early as grade 5 and have an opportunity to run your own company with classmates before completing senior high. You also have the opportunity to meet business leaders, gain self-confidence, and be recognized for your talents and accomplishments.

JA offers five education programs in the following areas:

(a) *Business basics:* Grades 5 to 6 students get a firsthand look at the business world and how it operates. The program is taught by consultants from the business world.

(b) *Project business:* Grades 8 to 9 students get an opportunity to participate in an activity-oriented program in which a business consultant works with the teacher to introduce basic economic concepts and principles of business. Students go on field trips to local businesses to experience the real world of business.

(c) *Applied economics:* Grades 11 to 12 students have a chance to learn micro and macro economics and how they apply to the operation of a student company.

(d) *Economics of staying in school:* This program is for students in grades 8 to 9 and promotes the importance of education via a series of classroom activities. Personal goals, living independently, and exploring career options are among the topics covered.

(e) *The company program:* This is an after-school activity for students in grades 10 to 12. It offers real-life business experience under the guidance of business advisers. Young people get to form their own company, develop a product or service, and operate the company right through to liquidation using a computerized financial record system.

To find out more about JA, write to:

Junior Achievement Inc.
One Education Way
Colorado Springs, CO 80906-4477
Tel: 1-800-265-0699 or
     (719) 540-8000

Junior Achievement of Canada
1 Westside Drive
Toronto, Ontario
M9C 1B2
Tel: 1-800-265-0699

2. Association of Collegiate Entrepreneurs

The Association of Collegiate Entrepreneurs (ACE) is an international non-profit organization dedicated to serving the needs of students interested in business ownership. ACE provides support, resources, and education to help students start successful ventures.

Through an international network of local campus-based chapters, ACE provides a forum for members to make friends with like-minded individuals. This network of friends motivates, inspires, and supports one another to achieve personal success.

Since many students cannot find business education in the classroom, ACE serves as a forum for self-discovery that exposes students to the benefits of free enterprise and entrepreneurship as a career option. This program should help students make informed decisions regarding their careers, and often students make the jump into their own business after participating in ACE events.

Local ACE chapter programs include the following:

(a) *Entrepreneurship awareness program:* This program promotes entrepreneurship among youth and the general public in a professional and exciting way. Chapters operate a number of programs including local media campaigns, high school speaking programs, public relations exercises, and other events. The development of the awareness campaign serves two functions for students. First, it familiarizes participating members with marketing and promotion skills, and second, it educates people about the benefits of entrepreneurship.

(b) *Entrepreneurship education, resource, and support programs*: Education programs are developed to reinforce members' innovative and creative instincts by providing insight, ideas, information, and advice relating to the start-up and operation of a business. Chapters conduct mentor programs, seminars, tours, conferences, and offer newsletters. These programs present an excellent opportunity for students to test their ideas with other like-minded students and help familiarize students with the dynamics of business communication and interaction.

(c) *Agency programs:* Student agencies are campus-based, chapter-run businesses or fundraising events that provide funds for the chapter and practical experience for participating members. These programs enable members to develop entrepreneurial, management, financial, marketing, and organization skills in a low-risk environment.

Interested students can contact ACE at:

180 Renfrew Drive, Suite 200
Markham, Ontario
L3R 8B7
Tel: 1-800-766-8169 (Canada only)
   (905) 470-5193 (outside Canada)

18
TROUBLE SHOOTING — PROBLEMS AND SOLUTIONS

The problems or failure of most student businesses arise either because the opportunity is not real, or the means required to pursue that opportunity are not available. Chances are that if you have followed this book well, your opportunity is real, you have ensured that the funds are available, and you now have the knowledge to pursue that opportunity.

Nevertheless, problems are a normal part of doing business. They often pose a special challenge for students, who are generally less experienced in the business world. The important thing to remember is that dealing with problems is part of your learning curve; every problem you face helps you do better in the future, whether you are successful at tackling the problem or not. When problems come up, start searching for solutions before they become insurmountable.

a. SOLUTIONS TO COMMON STUDENT-BUSINESS PROBLEMS

1. Lack of time

Are you able to spend time generating sales leads and do you follow up sales calls quickly? Are you available to manage job production and answer employee and customer concerns? Are you able to balance social life, business, and school?

If you are feeling overwhelmed, read some books on time management and follow the advice in chapter 16. Spend some time thinking about your priorities and how they can fit into your limited time

schedule. Most student entrepreneurs have to spend a great deal of time starting their business but can often take some time away to reorganize once it is running smoothly.

2. Poor market research or planning

Have you followed all the suggestions about planning and research in this book? Do your financial and income estimates represent what your business is capable of? Does your market really have the opportunity you thought it had? If so, what is preventing you from reaching that market?

Take a look at government and industry statistics and talk to your networking contacts to identify the difficulties. Once you understand what errors you made in your planning and research, reevaluate your business plan to deal with them. Correct any errors in your sales or expense forecasts. Then, use your own knowledge and feedback from your networking contacts to find ways to make your business profitable with these updated figures.

3. Trouble problem solving

No matter how experienced or educated you are, you cannot effectively solve all your business problems by yourself. When problems come up, get advice from others. Chapter 17 on networking gives you a great list of contacts who can help you. Also, listen to your employees for any feedback that may help you solve the problem.

4. Lack of experience

Lack of experience is part of a vicious circle. You can't do the job right until you've had the experience, and you can't get the experience if you don't have the opportunity to do the job. The only way to solve this problem is to try to get help from those who do have experience and try not to enter a field in which you have absolutely no experience. Aside from that, all you can do is try to learn what you can from your mistakes and apply that knowledge to make your next effort more profitable.

5. Lack of knowledge

The importance of having information is why doing a feasibility and market study was emphasized at the beginning of this book. Get more information and educate yourself about the area that is giving you problems. Use all your various personal and business contacts to gather information. Many government agencies can supply you with technical information.

6. Poor prioritizing

It is important that you become effective at prioritizing things in your business, social life, and studies. Do the most important things first. When there is time, do the less important things. However, never leave things until the last minute. Plan ahead and try to get started on things as early as possible. You should even plan to plan; that is, as your goals and plans are realized, re-evaluate your priorities and adjust your plans to meet those new priorities.

7. Difficulty making decisions

As an entrepreneur, you will face many key decisions, such as who to hire as well as what work to do, when, and how. If you are having difficulty making these decisions, small problems may build up to big ones and start to affect your business profitability and efficiency.

Solving these problems requires a combination of identifying, analyzing, and resolving current decision problems and bettering your decision-making skills for the future. Take some time and look at the problems. Ask your networking contacts for solutions.

Better decision-making skills come with education and experience. To speed up this learning process, get feedback from others with more education or experience than you. Again, your network of contacts is very useful here.

8. Poor response from advertising

The first thing to do if the response to your advertising is low or negative is to make sure you are targeting your advertising effectively; are you reaching your real target market? Choose the right advertising medium for that market and if you're not sure what the right one is, try several different media. Make sure your advertisements and presentations are competitive and professional; you won't get a positive response if people don't like your advertisements or feel that you are not capable of providing your service or product.

b. WHY YOU'RE NOT MEETING YOUR EXPECTATIONS

1. This is such a good idea — why is it not working?

Overconfidence is a typical problem for most new business owners. As long as you have researched your market properly and done a good feasibility study, your business will probably still be profitable even though it might not be as profitable as you thought. Sometimes when you have what you think is a good idea, it can be difficult to see the problems and you may overestimate the possibilities.

2. Low profits

If you are pricing your product or service competitively but are realizing low profits, you probably have a problem with your business efficiency. Make sure your product or service is priced competitively by following the steps laid out in chapter 11 on estimating and pricing your product and service. If this isn't the source of the problem, look at how you are producing your product or service. Are there areas that can be done more efficiently? Are employees working efficiently? Are they being overpaid for what they produce?

3. Frustration

Everyone gets frustrated when things are not going quite right and they cannot seem to change them. If your business takes longer to get started, it's easy to feel like giving up and not caring. The best advice here is to KEEP TRYING! Don't let things get you down. Keep looking for the causes of your frustration and problems and look for solutions, not reasons why you cannot solve them.

c. SELLING YOURSELF

Most problems related with selling yourself stem from doubts about your ability, fear of rejection, and shyness. Most of these problems have to be solved through experience, but there are a few things everyone should do regardless of their selling ability.

First, practice your selling skills with a friend or family member before dealing with customers, suppliers, or employees. Have them make sure you appear confident, professional, and enthusiastic.

Second, make sure you are as knowledgeable as possible about your field, your business strengths and weaknesses, and the strengths and weaknesses of your competitors. Do your research and work out the details to present a competitive price.

An important tip in selling yourself is to always let the customer know you want their business, that they are important, and that this job, no matter how small, is important to you. The best way to do this is to simply ask for the job.

If you still find that you have problems selling yourself, hire employees who have sales experience to help you until you get some practical experience. If you

are afraid of being rejected, or concerned about your shyness, practice your sales ability first and set up business meetings with just a few people so that you feel more comfortable. As you gain experience these skills will become easier and easier; you just have to give it a try, and stick with it until you have the experience and the confidence.

d. DEALING WITH EMPLOYEE PROBLEMS

Too often, small business owners are achievers who delegate poorly, overwork themselves, and expect everyone else to care about the business as much as they do. On the other hand, many employees are careless, unambitious, and not overly interested in the company's success. Many times, even if these differences are small, they can cause problems.

1. Conflicts between employees or between employees and the owner

The manager must try to work very closely with employees to develop unified objectives and a team approach. Try occasionally bringing coffee and donuts or having a staff party; people are more likely to talk about what's bothering them in a relaxed social setting. Having good communication amongst staff and between staff and you, the owner, is very important: When conflicts occur, staff will be more open to talk about the problems and less apt to let them affect their efficiency.

2. Hiring (and firing) staff

It is important to know exactly how many and what type of people your business needs. Consider making job descriptions so that employees know what is expected of them and you know what to expect of employees before hiring and training begins. Determine if the applicants really want the job and follow the guidelines set out in chapter 13 on employees. Taking these steps in the beginning will save you immeasurable frustration and stress later on.

However, if things aren't working out, first try to figure out why not. Ask yourself the following questions:

(a) Have I followed all the steps in chapter 13 about dealing with employees?

(b) Is the employee working effectively?

(c) Are my expectations of this employee reasonable?

(d) Have I trained this employee properly?

Once you understand the problem, it will be much easier to decide whether changes can solve the problem or if you have to find a new employee.

3. Motivating employees

Small student businesses have to be more productive to remain competitive than many larger or long-term businesses. Working only part-time or seasonally means that you must get everything out of your business that you can in the short time you have to run it. To do this, a student business owner must be able to motivate others to achieve their goals. Factors that often improve productivity include the following:

(a) *Security:* Employees want to feel confident that they can work a certain amount of hours each week and earn a certain amount of money each month. Thus, they are much less likely to be strongly motivated if they do not feel secure.

(b) *Open communication:* Employees need to know what to do and what's expected. They also have to get feedback — praise when they work hard and do well and help if they do something wrong.

(c) *Employee involvement in the business:* If employees have a say in quality control and can offer advice about procedure and management, employees are much more likely to feel proud and enthused about their work.

(d) *Benefits, promotions, and other returns for effort:* Employee return for effort put out must be what the employees expected in order for them to continue to produce work at a high level. This includes personal incentives, promotions, benefits, and amount of pay.

e. MANAGING CASH FLOW AND FINANCING PROBLEMS

1. Lack of cash

You can have the best business idea, but it won't get off the ground without sufficient cash. Read over chapter 7 on financing your business and look to family and friends or the bank for assistance to get things going until your business starts making a profit.

2. Finding funds for assets

Buying assets like vehicles or equipment that do not produce income is essential for your business. However, these assets drain cash and substantially increase the necessary initial investment. Keep costs down by renting, leasing, or borrowing any assets necessary for the business. Once you are underway, have begun to establish sales, and have a firm idea of your business's market potential, then consider purchasing the equipment.

Remember, as a student entrepreneur, you may not be running this business in two or five years. Spending less on non-income producing assets is wise because these assets may be difficult to resell after you close your business down. In general, buy what you absolutely need when you absolutely need it. Otherwise rent, borrow, or lease.

3. When to get a loan

When things are going well, everyone lends you money. In tough times when you really need cash, everyone wants their money back. Keep in mind that you have to pay back any credit you use and that taking credit means you have an obligation to your lenders. Obligations limit your ability to be flexible and may reduce your business success if you cannot meet them. This is not to say that using credit to start or expand your business is not a good idea. However, try to minimize it and always keep a portion of the profits in cash in case things start to get tight.

f. IF SCHOOL IS SUFFERING

1. Getting too busy

Being busy is what every entrepreneur hopes for; busy generally means money. Yet getting too busy can actually limit your ability to effectively manage your business and do well at school. Learn to delegate and plan ahead, taking every commitment — school, social, and business — into consideration. A three-month wall chart or time planner is often very effective and will help you keep from getting too busy.

2. Getting too big

If your business is getting too big, learn to delegate! Don't let quality diminish because of greed or haste. Try not to let administrative tasks overwhelm your time. Refer back to chapter 16 on time management and school.

g. EARLY SIGNS OF TROUBLE

It is very important that student entrepreneurs constantly attempt to identify problems and not wait until they build up or decrease profitability. Be active, not passive; identify problems and react to them in a timely manner. Apply effective and permanent solutions for the problem at hand. Short term solutions to problems invariably lead to more problems in the end. Remember, good management deals with all problems in a manner that improves the organization.

Failure to recognize problems early can often lead to frustration and financial difficulties. Try to foresee problems. Each week review your goals and assess whether your business is meeting them effectively. Use the following questions as a guide:

(a) *Is your business achieving its purpose?* Evaluate your successes or problems and analyze why you were successful and how you can avoid problems. Be sure that your business is meeting its goals and if it isn't, identify how to get things back on track.

(b) *Is the operation of the business running properly?* Are your business resources being used sufficiently and optimally? Are your employees productive? Are there any unneeded expenses?

(c) *Are the final results of the business profitable and are the customers more than satisfied with your product or service?* Keep a job project report (see chapter 14) to assess each job. Give customers comment sheets for their feedback.

(d) *Are sales falling?* If you find that your sales are beginning to drop, you should immediately start looking for the cause of the drop and attempt to develop a remedy to stop or at least slow down the sales decline. You may need to find a new way to reach your market.

(e) *Is your business getting more cost-effective and efficient as your experience increases?* If your business is getting less effective, then you are probably not managing your business as well as it could be managed.

(f) *What do your customers say about your service or product?* Make sure they are happy. If they have suggestions to do things better, seriously consider implementing their suggestions to help your business products or services retain their competitiveness.

(g) *What are your employees' attitudes and practices?* You want to be sure that your employees are doing their job with interest, motivation, and pride.

In general, if you see problems in your company, take action, assess the problems, and make changes to solve the problems and improve your business. This ensures your success and profitability as a student entrepreneur. When a problem arises, take the following steps to put things right:

(a) Take immediate action.

(b) Stop the problem.

(c) Find the cause of the problem.

(d) Decide how to prevent the problem from happening again.

(e) Get help if necessary to improve the aspects of your business that were creating the problem.

(f) Make sure the changes are both effective and permanent.

Sometimes you may find it difficult to solve serious problems on your own. Chapter 17 on networking has suggestions for outside contacts that can help you solve problems and mange your business.

Keep trying and don't give up! Try to identify your problems early on and look for reasons and ways to solve them rather than reasons why they cannot be solved. Everyone wants you to succeed; never be shy about asking people in your company or other business people for help.

APPENDIX
GOVERNMENT NAMES AND ADDRESSES

a. UNITED STATES

1. State departments offering business assistance

Alabama Development Office
401 Adams Avenue
Montgomery, Alabama 36130
Tel: (205) 242-0400

Alaska Department of Commerce and Economic Development
Division of Business Development
P.O. Box D
Juneau, Alaska 99811-0800
Tel: (907) 465-2017

Arizona Department of Commerce
3800 North Central, Suite 1500
Phoenix, Arizona 85012
Tel: (602) 280-1306

Arkansas Industrial Development Commission
Small Business Programs
One State Capital Mall
Little Rock, Arkansas 72201
Tel: (501) 682-5275

California Department of Commerce
Office of Small Business
801 K Street, Suite 1600
Sacramento, California 95814
Tel: (916) 324-1295

Colorado Small Business Center
Office of Business Development
1625 Broadway, Suite 1710
Denver, Colorado 80202
Tel: (303) 892-3809
Toll free in state: (800) 333-7798

Connecticut Department of Economic Development
Small Business Services
865 Brock Street
Hartford, Connecticut 06067-3405
Tel: (203) 258-4200

Delaware Development Office
99 Kings Highway
P.O. Box 1401
Dover, Delaware 19903
Tel: (302) 739-4271

District of Columbia Office of Business and Economic Development
717-14th Street, N.W., 10th Floor
Washington, D.C. 20005
Tel: (202) 727-6600

Florida Department of Commerce
Bureau of Business Assistance
443 Collins Building
107 W. Gaines Street
Tallahassee, Florida 32399-2000
Tel: (904) 487-9357

Georgia Department of Community Affairs
Community and Economic Development Section
1200 Equitable Building
100 Peachtree Street
Atlanta, Georgia 30303
Tel: (404) 656-3872

Hawaii Department of Business, Economic, Development, and Tourism
Business Services Division
Grosvenor Center, Mauka Tower
737 Bishop Street, Suite 1900
Honolulu, Hawaii 96804
Tel: (808) 586-2591

Idaho Department of Commerce
Economic Development Division
700 West State Street
Boise, Idaho 83720
Tel: (208) 334-2470

Illinois Department of Commerce and Community Affairs
SBDC Program
620 East Adams Street, 5th Floor
Springfield, Illinois 62701
Tel: (217) 524-5856

Indiana Small Business Development Corporation
One North Capitol Avenue, Suite 1275
Indianapolis, Indiana 46204
Tel: (317) 264-2820

Iowa Department of Economic Development
Small Business Bureau
200 East Grand Avenue
Des Moines, Iowa 50309
Tel: (515) 242-4758
Toll free in state: (800) 532-1216

Kansas Department of Commerce
400 S.W. 8th Street, 5th Floor
Topeka, Kansas 66603-3957
Tel: (913) 296-3480

Kentucky Cabinet for Economic Development
Division of Small Business
2300 Capital Plaza Tower
Frankfort, Kentucky 40601
Tel: (502) 564-7140

Louisiana Department of Economic Development
P.O. Box 94185
Baton Rouge, Louisiana 70804
Tel: (504) 342-5388

Maine Department of Economic and Community Development
Office of Business Development
State House Station #59
Augusta, Maine 04333
Tel: (207) 289-3153

Maryland Department of Economic and Employment Development
Division of Business Development
Redwood Towers, 10th Floor
217 East Redwood Street
Baltimore, Maryland 21202
Tel: (301) 333-6985

Massachusetts Office of Business Development
Business Services Division
Room 2101, One Ashburton Place
Boston, Massachusetts 02108
Tel: (617) 727-3206

Michigan Department of Commerce
P.O. Box 30004
Lansing, Michigan 48909
Tel: (517) 373-6241

Minnesota Small Business Assistance Office
900 American Center Building
150 East Kellogg Blvd.
St. Paul, Minnesota 55101
Tel: (612) 296-3871

Mississippi Department of Economic and Community Development
Business Assistance Division
P.O. Box 849
Jackson, Mississippi 39205
Tel: (601) 359-3552

Missouri Department of Economic Development
Business Development Section
Truman State Office Building
P.O. Box 118
Jefferson City, Missouri 65102
Tel: (314) 751-9055

Montana Department of Commerce
Business Development Division
1424 Ninth Avenue
Helena, Montana 59620
Tel: (406) 444-3923

Nebraska Department of Economic Development
P.O. Box 94666
301 Centennial Mall South
Lincoln, Nebraska 68509-4666
Tel: (402) 471-4167
Toll free in state: (800) 426-6505

Nevada Office of Small Business Commission on Economic Development
3770 Howard Hughes Parkway, Suite 295
Las Vegas, Nevada 89158
Tel: (702) 486-7282

New Hampshire Office of Business and Industrial Development
172 Pembroke Road
Concord, New Hampshire 03302-0856
Tel: (603) 271-2591

New Jersey Department of Commerce and Economic Development
Division of Development for Small
Businesses and Women and Minority
Businesses
20 West State Street, CN 835
Trenton, New Jersey 08625
Tel: (609) 292-3860

New Mexico Economic Development Department
Economic Development Division
1100 St. Francis Drive
Santa Fe, New Mexico 87503
Tel: (505) 827-0380

New York Department of Economic Development
Division for Small Business
1515 Broadway, 51st Floor
New York, New York 10036
Tel: (212) 827-6140

North Carolina Department of Commerce
Small Business Development
and Technology Center
4509 Creedmoor Road, Suite 201
Raleigh, North Carolina 27612
Tel: (919) 571-4154

North Dakota Department of Economic Development and Finance
1833 East Bismarck Expressway
Bismarck, North Dakota 58504
Tel: (701) 224-2810

Ohio Department of Development
Small Business Development Center
30 East Broadway Street
P.O. Box 1001
Columbus, Ohio 43266
Tel: (614) 466-2711
Toll free in state: (800) 848-1300

Oklahoma Department of Commerce
Small Business Assistance Office
6601 Broadway Extension
Oklahoma City, Oklahoma 73116
Tel: (405) 843-9770

Oregon Economic Development Department
Office of Small Business Assistance
775 Summer Street, N.E.
Salem, Oregon 97310
Tel: (503) 373-1241
Toll free in state: (800) 233-3306

Pennsylvania Department of Commerce
Office of Enterprise Development
401 Forum Building
Harrisburg, Pennsylvania 17120
Tel: (717) 783-8950

Puerto Rico Department of Commerce
P.O. Box S-4275
San Juan, Puerto Rico 00905
Tel: (809) 724-3290

Rhode Island Department of Economic Development
Business Development Division
7 Jackson Walkway
Providence, Rhode Island 02903
Tel: (401) 277-2601

South Carolina Office of Small and Minority Business Assistance
Edgar A. Brown Building
1205 Pendleton Street, Room 441
Columbia, South Carolina 29201
Tel: (803) 734-0562

South Dakota Governor's Office for Economic Development
711 East Wells Avenue
Pierre, South Dakota 57501-3369
Tel: (605) 773-5032

Tennessee Department of Economic and Community Development
320 6th Avenue North, 7th Floor
Nashville, Tennessee 37243-0405
Tel: (615) 741-2626
Toll free in state: (800) 872-7201

Texas Department of Commerce
816 Congress Avenue
P.O. Box 12728
Austin, Texas 78711
Tel: (512) 472-5059

Utah Department of Economic Development — Small Business
324 South State Street, Suite 500
Salt Lake City, Utah 84111
Tel: (801) 538-8775

Vermont Department of Economic Development
109 State Street
Montpelier, Vermont 05602
Tel: (802) 828-3221

Virgin Islands Small Business Development Agency
P.O. Box 6400
St. Thomas, Virgin Islands 00601
Tel: (809) 774-8784

Virginia Department of Economic Development
Small Business and Financial Services
P.O. Box 798
Richmond, Virginia 23206-0798
Tel: (804) 371-8100

Washington Department of Trade and Economic Development
Business Assistance Center
919 Lakeridge Way, S.W., Suite A
Olympia, Washington 98502
Tel: (206) 586-3021

West Virginia Governor's Office of Community and Industrial Development
Small Business Development Center Division
1115 Virginia Street East
Charleston, West Virgina 25301
Tel: (304) 348-2960

Wisconsin Department of Development
123 West Washington Avenue
P.O. Box 7970
Madison, Wisconsin 53707
Tel: (608) 266-7099

Wyoming Division of Economic and Community Development
Herschler Building, 2nd Floor West
Cheyenne, Wyoming 82002
Tel: (307) 777-7284

2. **Small Business Administration Information Office**

Many states operate small business development centers. Such centers are based at universities and offer programs that are organized and co-financed by Small Business Administration (SBA). Participating universities provide faculty and counseling to small business owners and offer seminars covering topics such as marketing, managing, and financing a small business. Check with your local SBA office for more information.

Small Business Administration (Central)
409 3rd Street, S.W.
Washington, D.C. 20416
Toll-free: (800) 827-5722

To order publications, write:
Small Business Administration Publications
P.O. Box 30
Denver, Colorado 20415

120

b. CANADA

The following are provincial government departments that give assistance or information to small business

Business Counselling Development
Branch
Sterling Place, 6th Floor
9940 - 106th Street
Edmonton, **Alberta**
T5K 2P6
Tel: (403) 427-3685

Ministry of Development, Trade and
Tourism
629 - 999 Canada Place
Vancouver, **British Columbia**
V6C 3E1
Tel: (604) 844-1800
Business Information Centre toll free:
1-800-972-2255

Department of Industry, Trade and
Tourism
155 Carlton Street, 4th Floor
Winnipeg, **Manitoba**
R3C 3H8
Tel: (204) 945-2456

Department of Development
P.O. Box 8700
St. John's, **Newfoundland**
A1B 4J6
Tel: (709) 729-5600

Department of Commerce and
Technology
P.O. Box 6000
Fredericton, **New Brunswick**
E3B 5H1
Tel: (506) 453-2965

Branch for Small Business
Tel: (506) 453-3890

Department of Economic Development
and Tourism
P.O. Box 1320
Yellowknife, **Northwest Territories**
X1A 2L9
Tel: (403) 873-7115

Department of Economic Development
Small Business Service Centre
#950 - 99 Wyse Road
Metropolitan Place
Dartmouth, **Nova Scotia**
B3A 4S5
Tel: (902) 424-5690

Small Business Ontario
900 Bay Street, 7th Floor
Toronto, **Ontario**
M7A 2E1
Toll free Business Start-up Hotline:
1-800-567-2345

Department of Industry
Shaw Building
P.O. Box 2000
Charlottetown, **Prince Edward Island**
C1A 7N8
Tel: (902) 368-4240

Ministere de l'Industrie et du Commerce
710 Place D'Youville
Quebec City, **Quebec**
G1R 4Y4
Tel: (418) 691-5950
For information on business programs:
Montreal: (514) 982-3010
Quebec City: (418) 691-5950

Economic Diversification and Trade
1919 Saskatchewan Drive, 5th Floor
Regina, **Saskatchewan**
S4P 3V7
Tel: (306) 787-1606

Business Development Office
Department of Economic Development
P.O. Box 2703
Whitehorse, **Yukon**
Y1A 2C6
Tel: (403) 667-3011

GLOSSARY

ACCOUNT

A statement of business transactions that tracks a company's assets, liabilities, and net worth.

ACCOUNTANT

A professional who manages and analyzes business records.

ACCOUNTS PAYABLE

Money owed to suppliers and others who have extended credit to a business. Accounts payable represents a liability.

ACCOUNTS RECEIVABLE

Money owed by customers and others to whom credit has been extended. Accounts receivable represents an asset.

ACCRUAL

A method of accounting that involves recording revenues and expenses when they occur, rather than when they are actually received.

ADVERTISING

Paid promotion of a business, usually in the form of telemarketing, fliers and posters, newspaper, radio, or TV advertisements.

ASSETS

Anything of value that a company owns, including money owing (accounts receivable). Assets equal liabilities plus net worth.

BALANCE

The value, positive or negative, of an account.

BALANCE SHEET

A list of assets, liabilities, and net worth in which assets are equal to liabilities plus net worth. Often referred to as a statement of financial position.

BOOKKEEPING

The procedure of keeping accounting records of a business's daily activities.

BREAK-EVEN POINT

The point at which expenses are equal to income. Beyond this point a company realizes a profit.

BUDGET

A statement of expected income and expenses over a given period of time.

BUSINESS CYCLE

A cycle which is the result of fluctuations in the economy; it includes prosperity, recession, depression, and recovery.

BUSINESS PLAN

A detailed list of goals set by the entrepreneur, describing the means and time frame by which to achieve them.

CAPITAL

Money and assets available for business activities.

CAPITALIZE

To treat as capital rather than as an expense; to take advantage of.

CASH FLOW

The amount of cash earned by, or available to, a business for investment, expenses, or expansion.

CEO

The chief executive officer or top official of a corporation.

COMPETITION

Companies that share the same market.

CONTRACT

A legal agreement between two or more parties specifying each party's responsibilities to meet determined business obligations.

CORPORATION

A company that exists as a separate legal entity from its owners.

COSIGNER

A person who jointly signs a loan or contract, pledging to meet the requirements of that loan or contract should the principal person be unable to fulfill his or her obligations.

COST

The amount of funds needed to produce a product or service.

COST OF GOODS

The cost of making a product, or the materials needed to produce a service.

CREDIT

Used in bookkeeping to record transactions, a credit is the opposite of a debit. Crediting an *asset account* decreases its value, while crediting a *liability account* increases its value.

CREDIT BUREAU

A bank or other organization which records, checks, and monitors the financial stability of a customer or business.

CREDIT PURCHASE

The purchase of products or services by a promise of future payment.

CREDIT RATING

A rating that denotes a person's or business's credit worthiness.

CREDIT SALE

Goods or services provided to a customer on the terms of promised future payment.

DEBIT

Used in bookkeeping to record transactions, a debt is the opposite of a credit. Debiting an *asset account* increases its value, while debiting a *liability account* decreases its value.

DEBT

Money owed to creditors.

DEFAULT

Not fulfilling an obligation or paying a debt within the specified time.

DEFICIT

When expenses are greater than income; the opposite of surplus.

DEMOGRAPHICS

Aspects such as the age, sex, income, and household composition of a particular target market.

DEPRECIATION

A loss of value due to use or age of a company's material assets.

ECONOMIES OF SCALE

The more you buy the less you pay: The theory that there is a decrease in the average cost per unit as the quantity of units bought or sold increases.

ECONOMY

The activities of producing and consuming that affect the income and buying patterns of particular groups of consumers.

EMPLOYEE

A person who works for a salary or hourly wage for a company, usually not owning an interest in the company.

EMPLOYER REMITTANCE

Income tax, social security payments, and other pay deductions required by the government and for which the employer is responsible for submitting.

ENTREPRENEUR

A person who starts and runs his or her own business.

EQUITY

Owner's equity is the value an owner has in his or her business. Equity capital is the owner's personal funds that are available to the business for investment or expenditure.

EXCISE TAX

A tax on the sale of particular commodities.

FINANCIAL PLAN

An estimate of a company's future income and expenses, broken down weekly, monthly, or yearly.

FINANCIAL STATEMENTS

Documents such as the income statement and balance sheet which detail a business's financial position.

FINANCING

Acquiring capital through loans and other means for the purpose of pursuing business activities.

FISCAL PERIOD

An accounting period, usually consisting of 12 months, and most commonly used for tax purposes.

FIXED EXPENSES

Business expenses that don't vary, regardless of the volume of business created.

FLOAT

Cash that is kept on hand by a retail business in order to make change for customers.

FRANCHISE

The right to use another company's ideas, brands, goods, or services under that company's name.

FRANCHISEE

The person or company buying the right to use another company's ideas, brands, goods, or services.

FRANCHISOR

The company selling the rights to use its ideas, brands, goods, or services.

GOODS

Tangible commodities.

GOODWILL

The value of intangible assets attained through previous marketing and business interactions.

GUARANTEE

A legal promise of quality or performance.

INCOME

Money received by the business from sales or investments.

INCOME STATEMENT

A formal financial document that serves as a summary of income and expenses and indicates profit or loss during a specified period of time.

INCOME TAX

A tax imposed by the government, usually calculated as a percentage of income.

INCUR

To take on the responsibility of, or become liable for, a debt.

INTANGIBLE ASSETS

An asset such as goodwill, which has no real value but which the company has as a result of operations.

INTEREST

An amount a lender charges to borrow money, it represents the profit a lender expects to make from the loan.

INVENTORY

The products, raw materials, or extra assets in the company's possession that are available for sale.

INVESTMENT

A spending of funds in the hope of realizing a profit.

INVOICE

A legal, itemized statement of goods or services sold (sales invoice) and purchased (purchase invoice).

JOURNAL

A record of a business's debits and credits, used for calculating profits, expenses, and taxes. Proper journal entries should have an accompanying receipt or invoice.

LAW OF DEMAND

The theory that market price and quantity demanded in the market vary inversely with one another.

LEARNING CURVE

A curve representing a decrease in cost of producing a good or service as a result of accumulated knowledge of how to produce the good or service more efficiently.

LEASE

The rental of equipment, facilities, or real estate for a specified amount of time and money. A lease agreement is usually longer than a rental agreement.

LIQUIDATE

The conversion of assets to cash.

LOAN

Money that a lender gives to a person or company for the purpose of making income via interest.

LOSS

A financial deficit. The result of income minus expenses; if negative, it is a loss.

MANAGEMENT

Administering and supervising a business's operations.

MARKET

A set of consumers.

MARKETING

The activities involved in finding, accessing, and informing a market of a business in order to sell a product or service.

MERCHANDISE

A company's inventory of products.

MINIMUM WAGE

A legally specified minimum rate of pay for labor in specific occupations.

NET

The amount of money that is left after all expenses have been deducted.

NETWORKING

Interacting with other people and organizations for the purpose of making contacts and developing business opportunities.

NET WORTH

The value of a business after all expenses have been deducted.

NICHE

A small market segment, often isolated from competition by degree of specialization or size.

NSF CHECKS

Not Sufficient Fund checks are those checks that are returned by the bank because the person writing the check does not have enough money in his or her account to cover the check. The bank usually charges an additional service fee for this transaction.

OPERATING COSTS

Costs created by the production of business products or services.

OUTPUTS

The goods and services that result from the process of production.

OVERHEAD

The fixed costs of operating a business. They often include rent and lease payments.

PARTNERSHIP

A legal business relationship consisting of two or more people who jointly take the responsibility for ownership of a business.

PLAN

A decision to pursue and obtain a specific goal using a prescribed method.

PRIME RATE

The interest banks may charge their most credit worthy or largest customers.

PRINCIPAL

A person who is primarily responsible for a business enterprise, or the original amount of an investment put up by the investor in cash.

PROACTIVE

Anticipation of problems and the drive to avoid or solve them before they occur. The opposite of reactive.

PRODUCT

The goods a company produces for sale.

PRODUCTIVITY

The output produced per unit of input.

PROFIT

The financial gain realized by doing business. The result of income minus expenses; if positive, it is a profit.

PROFIT AND LOSS STATEMENT

A document showing total revenue of a company and total expenses incurred to generate that revenue. The difference between revenue and expenses is a profit if it is positive, and a loss if it is negative.

PROFIT MARGIN

The sale price minus the total costs.

PRO FORMA

Projected financial statements that reflect estimates for future performance.

R AND D

Research and development; the costs associated with the creation and development of new products or services.

REACTIVE

A response to problems after they happen; the opposite of proactive.

RECESSION

A point in the business cycle of declining economic activity.

RENT

The use of equipment, facilities, or real estate for a specified amount of time and money.

RETAIL

The selling of goods or services to the end user.

SALES TAX

A tax imposed on the sale of a product or service, calculated as a percentage of the selling price. It is charged to the customer and remitted to the government by the seller. The rate of sales tax varies, depending on the location of your business.

SATURATED MARKET

A market that has a large number of competitors competing for a specific product or service in all available areas.

SERVICE BUSINESS

A business that deals in advice or performs a task requiring labor.

SOLE PROPRIETORSHIP

A business owned by one person.

SURPLUS

An amount that is leftover; what is left when income is higher than expenses, or the extra inventory after a certain period.

TANGIBLE

Something that can be evaluated at an actual value. A tangible asset includes things such as equipment, vehicles, and buildings.

TARGET MARKET

Potential customers identified by such characteristics as age, income, and personal interests.

TAX

A charge levied on goods, income, or property by the government.

TERMS OF SALE

The conditions under which a company does business. It usually refers to means and form of payment, and specifies the time in which the account must be paid.

UNEMPLOYMENT INSURANCE

A government-administered plan to compensate for loss of income due to lack or loss of work.

VALUE ADDED

The value of a firm's output minus the value of the inputs that it purchases from other businesses; the increase in value of materials due to assembly into a product.

VARIABLE EXPENSES

Costs that vary directly with changes in production, sales, or outputs.

VOLUME

The amount of business a company does, often measured in the number of units sold or hours of service provided.

WHOLESALE

The selling of goods for the purpose of reselling.

WORKERS' COMPENSATION

A government-administered fund that compensates employees for an injury or disability that is the result of employment.

WORKING CAPITAL

Current assets minus current liabilities.

OTHER TITLES IN THE SELF-COUNSEL
BUSINESS SERIES

PREPARING A SUCCESSFUL BUSINESS PLAN
A practical guide for small business
by Rodger Touchie, B.Comm., M.B.A.

At some time, every business needs a formal business plan. Whether considering a new business venture or rethinking an existing one, an effective plan is essential to success. From start to finish, this working guide outlines how to prepare a plan that will win potential investors and help achieve business goals.

Using worksheets and a sample plan, readers learn how to create an effective plan, establish planning and maintenance methods, and update their strategy in response to actual business conditions. $14.95

Contents include:

- The basic elements of business planning
- The company and its product
- The marketing plan
- The financial plan
- The team
- Concluding remarks and appendixes
- The executive summary
- Presenting an impressive document
- Common misconceptions in business planning
- Your business plan as a tangible asset

BASIC ACCOUNTING FOR THE SMALL BUSINESS
Simple, foolproof techniques for keeping your books straight and staying out of trouble
by Clive Cornish, C.G.A.

Having bookkeeping problems? Do you feel you should know more about bookkeeping, but simply don't have time to take a course? Do you wish that the paperwork in your business could be improved, but you don't know where or how to start?

This book is a down-to-earth manual on how to save your accountant's time and your time and money. Written in clear, everyday English, not in accounting jargon, this guide will help you and your office staff keep better records.

Inside you will find illustrations of sample forms and instructions on how to prepare all the records you will need to keep, including:

- Daily cash sheet
- Cash summary
- Statement ledger
- Payables journal
- Synoptic journal
- Payroll book
- Income statement
- Trial balance
- Columnar work sheet

U.S. ed. $7.95, Canadian ed. $8.95

THE ADVERTISING HANDBOOK FOR SMALL BUSINESS

Make a big impact with a small budget

by Dell Dennison

If you want more bang from your advertising dollar, this book is for you. It explains, step by step, what advertising is, how it works, and, most important, what will work best for *your* small business. Worksheets and samples explain advertising concepts in easy-to-understand detail.

The first edition of *The Advertising Handbook* received the Washington Press Association's Communicator Award for best instructional book of the year in 1991. This second edition has been updated, expanded, and made even more useful with the addition of many new worksheets to help you develop the most effective advertising campaign for your business. $10.95

Some of the topics discussed include:

- Identifying your best target audience
- Aiming your message to hit that target dead center
- The importance of positioning
- How to decide whether to hire an ad agency
- How to do your own low-cost research
- Effective copywriting and design techniques
- Producing your own advertising with desktop publishing
- When and how to use radio, television, print, and other types of media
- How to write a press release